Those Damned YANKEES

The Not-So-Great History of Baseball's Evil Empire

Those Damned YANKEES

The Not-So-Great History of Baseball's Evil Empire

By Clarke Canfield

ISLANDPORT PRESS

Islandport Press Inc.
P.O. Box 10
Yarmouth, Maine 04096
islandport@islandportpress.com
www.islandportpress.com

ISBN: 0-9763231-2-5
Library of Congress Control Number: 2005925938

First edition published June 2005

Book design by Islandport Press Inc.
Cover design by Karen F. Hoots / Mad Hooter Design
Back cover photo by The Associated Press

DEDICATION

To my son, Eli. Should he grow up to be a Red Sox slugger,
may he beat the Yankees over and over again.

TABLE OF CONTENTS

YANKEE LOATHING KNOWS NO BOUNDS

If you're a Boston Red Sox fan, there was nothing sweeter than watching the Sox win the 2004 World Series—unless it was watching the Sox beat the New York Yankees to get there.

But Red Sox fans aren't the only ones with a healthy dislike—hatred, loathing, abhorrence, detestation, call it what you want—for the players in pinstripes. There are millions of Yankee haters around the world who took as much satisfaction in watching the Yankees lose as they did in seeing the Red Sox win. The Yankees are unquestionably the most hated team in baseball history.

The Yankees are to baseball what Wal-Mart and General Motors are to the business world. They are a bloodless, soulless organization with all the warmth of an accounting ledger's bottom line. They are vain and egotistical, with as much modesty as a stripper.

The franchise has a bottomless pit of money—not to mention arrogance, smugness, narcissism and self-importance. It is with good reason that the Yankees are known as baseball's Evil Empire.

The Yankees celebrate the power of the almighty dollar, and attempt to use its seductive power to buy championships. They make heroes out of drunks, convicts, braggarts and boors. The owner acts like a czar.

The Yankees are anything but the everyman's team. They are for the privileged, luxury-box corporate crowd. We couldn't agree more with the late Chicago newspaper columnist Mike Royko, who said, "Hating the Yankees is as American as pizza pie, unwed mothers, and cheating on your income tax."

This book is for the people all over the globe who hate the Yankees and all they stand for. It takes a hard look—perhaps a little tongue-in-cheek—at the most illuminating moments in Yankee history, at least in the eyes of Yankee haters. It looks at the lowlights in Yankee history by examining the team's infamous players, feats, seasons, and exploits both on and off the field.

Make no mistake about it: This book savors anything and everything that casts embarrassment and shame on the Yankee franchise. Here's to the Yankees, a deserving target of ridicule if there ever was one.

Clarke Canfield
South Portland, Maine
May 2005

WARMING UP

AP Photo

Previous page—Bill Lee throws a pitch against the New York Yankees in July 1975 at Shea Stadium. Behind his pitching, the Red Sox won the game, 1–0.

Now Pitching . . .

Bill "Spaceman" Lee

Revenge is sweetest when dished out cold!

This will be as cold as walking naked on the dark side of the moon. Here is a vitriolic diatribe of a free radical not-so-deep thinker. Ramblin' down I-95, trying to avoid another mid-Atlantic nor'easter, what else would a southern California boy be doing in the face of winter? Run, Billy, run! Don't get me wrong, I like winter and snow, they both keep the hordes away from my halfway house in Vermont.

They say the Inuit have a hundred different words for snow. I, being a fifth generation of Baja, Oregon, have just two adjectives for snow. Neither can be used in this narrative.

I'm heading to Florida to play ball again, this time with Twig, Billy Milliken, and Butch Hall, a few hard-drinking "maniacs" kinda like me. Diana says I'm only happy when I'm playing ball, kicking ass and taking names—that's all I'm good for sometimes. I'm also not bad with a Sachs-Dolmar doing a chain-saw renovation of my kitchen—not exactly the tool of choice for a finishing carpenter.

I digress; let's get back on the path of revenge, kicking ass and taking names. A wise man from Oklahoma said he never met a man he didn't like, but he never met Graig Nettles or any other member of the Yankee teams of the seventies. What a team to hate: Billy Martin, Graig Nettles, Reggie Jackson, Mickey Rivers, Graig Nettles (I hate him a lot).

Thurman Munson—no, we can't say a disparaging word against the dead, can we? Yeah, yes we can—he was an arrogant prick. But then if the Red Sox had traded me instead of Sparky Lyle to the Yankees for Danny Cater, I would have fit in perfectly with that team, since I am a cocky prick, too.

I want to extend my congratulations to the 2004 Boston Red Sox and their never-to-be-duplicated victory. For the first time in Yankee lore, they wear the horns of the most ignominious defeat in baseball, and no one enjoyed it more than me. I was blessed to be in Maui at that time, marrying off my eldest daughter, Caitlin, a more beautiful wedding you will never see.

A WISE MAN FROM OKLAHOMA SAID HE NEVER MET A MAN HE DIDN'T LIKE, BUT HE NEVER MET GRAIG NETTLES OR ANY OTHER MEMBER OF THE YANKEE TEAMS OF THE SEVENTIES.

Thank you, Charles Laquidara, the greatest WBCN rock DJ in Boston, and my longtime friend. Thank you for keeping me in front of your TV and not letting me miss a single pitch. Those four victories made Maui into the western extreme of Red Sox Nation.

I recommend Maui for all Red Sox playoff games. You awaken to first light refreshed, have a cup of organic Kona gold, walk to the beach, put on your snorkel and fins, commune with the green turtles and hundreds of species of tropical fish. After a nice brunch we would head up the volcano to Chuck's for Reposado Margaritas and sit down to a wide-screen Yankee ass-kickin'.

Many high-fives later, and a few "We live for one game," we venture down the Hana Highway to a sports bar in Kahului for a little chest-puffing before Yankee fans. When we were down 1–3, the split in the bar was 50/50. By game six it was 80/20, and when we had staged the greatest comeback in playoff history, the Yankee fans in the bar had shrunk like a testicle dipped in a March brook in Maine. Yes, cold revenge.

The 2004 Red Sox were like therapy. The 487 New Englanders who passed away that night, in rest homes and local hospitals, all died with smiles on their faces—at least that is what the eyewitness accounts said.

This team lifted a weight off of my shoulders. The weight of a hanging curveball, served to Tony Perez, the weight of not winning Game 2 in '75. The weight of leaving the Red Sox against my will. I have wanted revenge. The Chinese say, "When you seek revenge, you dig two graves!" Now, as I get closer to Florida, the sound in my ears gets louder.

As I listen closer, I hear Gordon Lightfoot singing, "I don't know what went wrong, but the feeling's gone and I just can't get it back."

BILL "SPACEMAN" LEE
WINTER 2005
SOMEWHERE ALONG INTERSTATE 95
BETWEEN VERMONT AND FLORIDA

William Francis "Spaceman" Lee compiled a career record of 119–90 with an ERA of 3.62 while pitching for the Boston Red Sox (1969–1978) and Montreal Expos. He remains the 13th-winningest pitcher (94–68) in Red Sox history and the third-winningest left-hander. He started Games 2 and 7 of the famed 1975 World Series against the Reds. He is well known in New England for nicknaming Don Zimmer the Gerbil, and for hating the New York Yankees as much as anyone. He now lives in Vermont, and his latest book, Have Glove Will Travel: Adventures of a Baseball Vagabond, *was released in 2005.*

First Inning

Previous page—Despite the presence of future Hall of Famers Babe Ruth (left) and Lou Gehrig, shown here in 1933, their Yankee teams in 1925 and 1928 suffered two of the most lopsided losses in franchise history.

GAMES

Despite megawealth and lineups filled with obscenely paid home-run sluggers and pitching aces, the New York Yankees have bungled numerous games over the years—looking more like Little Leaguers just learning to play than big leaguers making gazillions of dollars a year. Sometimes it seems the Yankees just don't show up. Too busy preening in front of the mirror or rereading fawning clips from a lapdog New York media that specializes in creating Yankee myths and false idols? Quite possibly.

There are such great games in Yankee history dating to the start of the franchise and continuing throughout the twentieth century and into the twenty-first century. These mid-season games bring some special joy to the long baseball year.

2004
CLEVELAND INDIANS 22
NEW YORK YANKEES 0

AUGUST 31, 2004—Despite a $183-million payroll and an All Star-studded lineup, the Yankees looked like the Bad News Bears when they played the Cleveland Indians on August 31. Going into the game, the Indians had lost eight straight at Yankee Stadium, but the scoreboard keeper's head was spinning that night as the hits and runs just kept on coming in a 22–0 trouncing—the worst beating in Yankee history.

With owner George Steinbrenner and 51,777 fans looking on, Cleveland scored three in the first, three in the second and three more in the third. Then a six-run fifth inning was followed by a single run in the sixth to make it 16–0. The icing on the cake came in the ninth when the Indians batted around, scoring six more times to produce the final outcome.

"THE ONLY THING YOU CAN SAY IS THAT IT ONLY COUNTS AS ONE," SAID JOE TORRE, YANKEE MANAGER. "THEY SURE BEAT OUR BRAINS OUT RIGHT FROM THE FIRST INNING ON, AND WE DIDN'T HAVE AN ANSWER."

Fans booed early and often during the game in which Omar Vizquel of the Indians tied an American League record with six hits in nine innings, missing the record by flying out in the ninth. In addition to it being the Yankees' worst rout ever, the game also matched the biggest modern-day shutout margin in the Major Leagues, set in 1975 when the Pittsburgh Pirates embarrassed the Chicago Cubs 22–0 in Chicago. The Yankees could take some solace in that the old Indianapolis Hoosiers lost to the Phillies 24–0 way back in 1887.

"There's a certain element of embarrassment, no question," manager Joe Torre said after the game.

	1	2	3	4	5	6	7	8	9	R	H	E
Cleveland	3	3	3	0	6	1	0	0	6	22	22	1
New York	0	0	0	0	0	0	0	0	0	0	5	0

CLE- Westbrook (W 12–6)
NYY- Vazquez (L 12–8)
HR: Yankees, NONE; CLE, Crisp (13), Martinez (21), Gerut (10)

1925
DETROIT TIGERS 19
NEW YORK YANKEES 1

JUNE 17, 1925—The Yankees were nothing special in 1925, finishing 16 games below .500 and 28.5 games out of first place. They were even less special on a mid-June day when they were clobbered by the Detroit Tigers, 19–1, at the time the franchise's worst mauling.

The Tigers—a team that included future Hall of Famer Charlie Gehringer and an aging Ty Cobb—scored 13 runs in the sixth inning alone, 11 before they even made an out. It took 49 minutes to play the top of the sixth, an inning that featured seven walks and six hits.

The 19 runs by the Tigers stood as the most runs scored by a Yankee opponent at Yankee Stadium until the Cleveland Indians scored 22 in 2004.

1928
NEW YORK YANKEES 6
CLEVELAND INDIANS 24

JULY 29, 1928—The Yankees' 1928 lineup featured Babe Ruth, Lou Gehrig, and Bob Meusel, who finished one-two-three in RBIs in the league that year. But that wasn't enough to scare off the Indians on July 29.

On that day at old League Park in Cleveland, the seventh-place Tribe handed pennant-bound New York the beating of its franchise history, 24–6. Twenty-four remains the most runs scored in one game against the Yankees.

The Indians scored eight in the first inning and nine more in the second off star pitcher George Pipgras before the Yankees knew what hit them. Cleveland's Johnny Hodapp became the first American League player to get two hits in an inning twice in a game—hitting two singles in both the second and sixth innings. He also doubled, stole a base and took part in two double plays.

1977
TORONTO BLUE JAYS 19
NEW YORK YANKEES 3

SEPTEMBER 10, 1977—The Toronto Blue Jays' Roy Howell drove in nine runs with a single, two doubles and two home runs as the Blue Jays hammered the Yankees, 19–3, at Yankee Stadium.

Howell's 13 total bases and nine RBIs still stand as Blue Jay records. His five hits and four extra-base hits are still tied for first in franchise history.

For the Yankees, Catfish Hunter took the loss to finish his season at 9–9.

1907
NEW YORK YANKEES 0
CHICAGO WHITE SOX 15

1950
CHICAGO WHITE SOX 15
NEW YORK YANKEES 0

JULY 15, 1907 and MAY 5, 1950—The Yankees were still called the Highlanders and played their home games at Hilltop Park when they traveled to Chicago to take on the White Sox on July 15, 1907.

The game at South Side Park ended in what was then the franchise's worst defeat, 15–0. It was such a one-sided drubbing that the lopsided score stood up as the worst shutout in Yankee history for 97 years.

However, 43 years later the White Sox did paste the Yankees

HOWEVER, FORTY-THREE YEARS LATER THE WHITE SOX PASTED THE YANKEES 15–0 FOR A SECOND TIME. THIS GAME, THOUGH, WAS EVEN MORE EMBARRASS-ING—IT TOOK PLACE AT YANKEE STADIUM.

15–0 for a second time. This game, though, was even more embarrassing—it took place at Yankee Stadium.

2003
HOUSTON ASTROS 8
NEW YORK YANKEES 0

JUNE 11, 2003—At Yankee Stadium, the Houston Astros truly used a team effort to no-hit the Yankees, tossing the first six-pitcher no-hitter in Major League history.

Starter Roy Oswalt lasted but an inning before leaving with a strained groin, but he and five other hurlers set a record for the most pitchers used in a no-hitter, besting the previous record of four.

It was the first time in 45 years the Yankees had been victims of a no-hitter. To add insult, the Yankees even struck out four times in the eighth inning. Manager Joe Torre called the game "an inexcusable performance."

1990
CHICAGO WHITE SOX 4
NEW YORK YANKEES 0

JULY 1, 1990—Before a crowd of 30,642 at old Comiskey Park, Yankee starter Andy Hawkins was having the game of his life. He took a no-hitter into the bottom of the eighth inning— then, suddenly, the bottom fell out.

With two outs, the Yankees' Mike Blowers misplayed Sammy Sosa's routine grounder for an error, and Hawkins promptly walked two to load the bases—still maintaining his no-hitter. The next batter, Robin Ventura, stroked a lazy fly ball that Jim Leyritz dropped, clearing the bases and giving the Sox a 3–0 lead. The next batter hit a fly ball that Jesse Barfield lost in the sun, scoring Ventura and making it 4–0.

The Yankees failed to score in the top of the ninth, giving the White Sox a 4–0 win and giving Hawkins an eight-inning no-hitter and a lost game. It was the first time since 1964 that a Major League pitcher had lost a no-hitter, and represented the largest margin of defeat of any pitcher who tossed a no-hitter and lost.

"HATING THE YANKEES IS AS AMERICAN AS PIZZA PIE, UNWED MOTHERS, AND CHEATING ON YOUR INCOME TAX."

—MIKE ROYKO, COLUMNIST

NOW BATTING . . .

DALE ARNOLD

Hate is a four-letter word. In our house, hate is taboo. Our children have been taught, from a very early age, that there is no room for hate, and they are not even allowed to use the word.

Now that all the politically correct mumbo jumbo has been dispensed with . . . I hate the Yankees.

I hate the word, I hate the team, I hate the concept and I hate the nearly pathological success rate of the Major League Baseball team that calls the Bronx their home. I hate the Yankees.

Seinfeld once said that we are all just reduced to rooting for laundry, but I honestly believe that it is possible to despise laundry as well. I hate those caps with the overlapping letters, N and Y. How do you actually tell which letter comes first? Oh, that's right, it's the Yankees, and everyone knows. I hate pinstripes. Even knowing of their naturally slimming effect does little to reduce my level of antipathy. My hate is inbred enough that I can't even allow myself to buy a simple, navy pinstripe suit. I hate the Yankees.

I hate their 39 pennants, 44 playoff appearances and 26 World Championships. I guess, in fairness, it's not their World Series titles I hate as much as it is the effect those World Championships have on the fandom of the Yankees. I hate their egotistical, chest-thumping, all-encompassing, pig-headed, never-ending, jaw-wagging, nerve-grinding, bottom-feeding, self-aggrandizing sense of self-importance and entitlement. I hate the Yankees.

I hate every player who has ever worn a Yankee uniform. I've respected a few—very few—but I've hated them all, even those Yankees who have also worn a Red Sox uniform during their careers. From Babe Ruth to Luis Tiant to Sparky Lyle to Wade Boggs to Roger Clemens, my feelings have been the same. They were good guys and good to great players when they played in Boston, but they were bums the minute the pinstripes went on. They ceased being bums the minute those same pinstripes came off. I hate the Yankees.

I hate Yankee Stadium. I hate that it's called the House that Ruth Built, because we all know that he built Fenway first, when it comes right down to it, but we never call our field that. I hate the short right-field porch, I hate the left-field bleachers (especially after Aaron Boone's home run in ALCS game 7 in 2003). I hate the aura, I hate the history, I hate the monuments, I hate the giant baseball bat outside, and I hate the sense of dread every Red Sox fan has ever felt when their first batter steps into the box in the Bronx. I hate the Yankees.

I love New York, but I hate the Yankees. In their entire history, from 1901 when they were actually called the Baltimore Orioles, through 1912 when they were the New York Highlanders, up until today, I've rooted for them exactly once. That was when President George W. Bush walked to the Yankee Stadium mound

I HATE THEIR EGOTISTICAL, CHEST-THUMPING, ALL-ENCOMPASSING, PIG-HEADED, NEVER-ENDING, JAW-WAGGING, NERVE-GRINDING, BOTTOM-FEEDING, SELF-AGGRANDIZING SENSE OF SELF-IMPORTANCE AND ENTITLEMENT. I HATE THE YANKEES.

on October 30, 2001, to deliver the ceremonial first pitch in the third game of the first World Series after the events of 9/11. I cried like a baby, then cheered like a schoolgirl when he delivered a strike over the heart of the plate. I saw how important the game was to the people of New York, how baseball could help in the healing of a city and a nation, and I rooted for the Yankees for the first and only time in my life. I loved my country, New York City and the heroes honored before and during the game. I admit that those feelings can still bubble to the surface when I see that American bald eagle fly in from center field, when Ronan Tynan sings "God Bless America," or when Bob Shepard welcomes us all to Yankee Stadium. Then I come to my senses and remember who and what I am—I am a New Englander, born and bred, a baseball fan and a Red Sox fan, and I hate the Yankees.

I used to hate the months of September and October because of the Yankees. I hated that Reggie Jackson was Mr. October and all of my favorite players were only fit to be called Mr. May. I hated that every spring, every Red Sox fan was convinced that this was the year, and every Yankee fan smugly smiled and pointed to the fall months on the calendar, secure in the knowledge that they would be playing baseball after the leaves had turned, while Red Sox fans got their annual early start on the hot stove season. I hate the Yankees.

I hate that no matter what any team in baseball does to draft properly, nurture adequately and develop fundamentally, the Yankees can write a check and buy any good player they want. I hate that every Yankee fan thinks it's a right of divine providence that they get every free agent that matters and that every team in baseball should trade any player to New York that catches a Yankee fan's eye. I hate that every representative for every free agent begins his off-season effort with a phone call to the Yankees, because even if the Yankees don't want that player, at least it drives up the price for the team that's left with New York's castoffs. I hate the Yankees.

13

I hope I've left no gray area here. I grew up in the great state of Maine where we like red tide and nor'easters more than the Yankees. I hate the Yankees, I hate the Yankees, I hate the Yankees.

Who would I like to see the Red Sox play next October for an American League Championship and a berth in the World Series? Oh, I would love the Yankees.

Dale Arnold, who grew up in Maine, has served as the voice for the old Maine Mariners, New Jersey Devils, New England Patriots, New England Revolution and Boston Bruins. He is the only person to call play-by-play for at least one game for each of the five Boston professional teams: Red Sox, Patriots, Bruins, Celtics and Revolution. He is currently a co-host of a sports talk show on Sports Radio WEEI 850 AM in Boston. Dale, his wife Susan, son Taylor, and daughters Alysha and Brianna, live in Wrentham, Massachusetts. They hate the Yankees.

SECOND INNING

AP Photo

Previous page—The mid-sixties teams of Mickey Mantle (shown here at Yankee Stadium in 1965) were some of the worst in Yankee history. From 1965 to 1969, the Yankees finished a collective 120 games out of first place, including a last-place finish in 1965. Mantle retired after the 1968 season.

SEASONS

Lost among the propaganda of the media and the smug arrogance of Yankee fans lies the fact that the team has actually failed during the regular season. In fact, the Empire has not only submitted some wire-to-wire stinkers, but even coughed up a division lead or two in the process. Imagine that! The Yankees' regular season struggles started in earnest in 1908 when the team posted a 57–103 record. Let the good times roll.

1908
100 LOSSES AND COUNTING

If nothing else, the New York Highlanders were consistently inconsistent their first five years in New York after moving from Baltimore. In 1904, they posted a .609 winning percentage and finished 1.5 games out of first place. The following year they finished below .500 and far out of the pennant race.

In 1908, they stunk it up bad, finishing with a 51–103 record and were officially inducted into the "100 Club," that special fraternity of teams that lose more than 100 games. The 1908 Yankees set team records that still stand to this day for most losses in a season (103), most home losses in a season (47), and most losses in a month (24, in July). The 1908 edition also holds team records for most consecutive road losses (12) and fewest runs scored in a season (459).

"Smilin' Al" Orth, who won 27 games in 1906 and 14 in 1907, wasn't smiling so much in 1908 as his record fell to 2–13. Jack Chesbro, who was 23–17 and 10–10 the previous two seasons, lost 20 games. First baseman Hal Chase had a career-worst .257 batting average. "Wee Willie" Keeler, the 5-foot-4-inch hitting whiz who came to the Yankees in 1903 after hitting as high as .424 in the 1890s while playing in the National League, was relegated to part-time status and slumped to .263. Manager Clark Griffith was fired after the season.

The team's futility showed in the standings. The team finished with a .331 winning percentage, and ended the season in last place, 31.5 games out. (That year, Cleveland, Chicago and Detroit remained in the pennant race until the last day, with the Tigers winning the pennant by a half-game because they weren't required to make up a rainout from earlier in the season.)

The Yankees' ineptitude was also evident in the stands; only 305,500 fans showed up for the entire year. It was the worst attendance since the team's inaugural year in New York five years earlier, and a 30 percent drop from 1906.

Even worse, the team drew just a third as many fans as the swaggering New York Giants—the reigning kings of New York baseball.

1912
THE WORST YANKEE TEAM EVER

If the 1908 season was a good one for Yankee haters, the 1912 campaign was heaven.

The 1912 club is held up by many as the worst in franchise history. New York finished in last place with a record of 50–102, for a .329 winning percentage that was good enough to finish—don't laugh now—55 games behind the World Series Champion Boston Red Sox. Several Yankee records set that year still stand, including fewest road wins in a season (19) and most road losses (58).

Hal Chase, supposedly the best-fielding first baseman in the league, committed 27 errors—and all the while, rumors swirled that he was throwing games. Canadian righthander Russ Ford, who was a combined 48–17 in 1910 and 1911, fell to 13–21—despite the help of his famed "emery pitch," so named because he scuffed up the ball with emery paper.

THE FANS—THE FEW WHO SHOWED UP—HAD LITTLE TO CHEER ABOUT. THE TEAM'S ATTENDANCE WAS ONLY 242,194—BARELY 3,000 A GAME.

Yankee pitchers surrendered an American League-high 28 home runs and posted the league's highest ERA (4.13). The hitters managed but 18 homers, third worst among the 16 teams in all the Majors.

The fans—the few who showed up— had little to cheer about. The team's attendance was only 242,194 fans—barely 3,000 a game. The draw has not fallen so low since. Meanwhile, the rival Boston Red Sox, opening brand-new Fenway Park, finished in first place by 14 games and went on to win the team's second World Series title, beating the New York Giants 4 games to 3, with 1 tie. (During the 1912 season,

---

1912 American League Standings

Team	W	L	T	GB
Boston*	105	47	2	—
Washington	91	61	2	14
Philadelphia	90	62	1	15
Chicago	78	76	4	28
Cleveland	75	78	2	30.5
Detroit	69	84	1	36.5
St. Louis	53	101	3	53
New York	**50**	**102**	**1**	**55**

* World Series Champion

"Smoky" Joe Wood led the way for the Boston Red Sox, finishing the year with 34 wins and a 1.91 ERA. Tris Speaker was spectacular in the field and at the plate, hitting .383 and leading the league with 10 home runs. In the World Series, Wood outdueled Christy Mathewson in game 7 to win the championship.)

When the season came to a merciful end, the team fired manager Harry Wolverton, marking a Steinbrenner-esque fifth managerial change in five years.

1933
THE YANKEES BLOW A SIX-GAME LEAD

Fresh off a World Series sweep of the Chicago Cubs and the team's second-best season on record, the Yankees were feeling giddy about themselves when the 1933 campaign got under way.

Their lineup featured Babe Ruth and Lou Gehrig, who would end the season with a combined 66 homers and 242 RBIs. It was the Babe's last big year and his penultimate season with the Yankees. Meanwhile, Tony Lazzeri knocked in 104 runs, and Ben Chapman and Bill Dickey had 98 and 97 RBIs, respectively.

The Yankees started the season strong, winning their first seven games and ending May with a 25–13 record. On June 6, after sweeping two consecutive doubleheaders against Philadelphia and Boston, the Yankees found themselves in first by six games over the Washington Senators. The Yankees had won seven straight and 11 of 12.

But the season was still young, as the Yankees would soon learn. The team folded in June, losing seven of its next nine games, while Washington went on a tear, winning 15 of 16. The Senators not only got back in the race, they took the lead before July even rolled around.

By the time the 1933 season ended, the Yankees stood seven games in back of Washington, a turnaround of 13 games since early June.

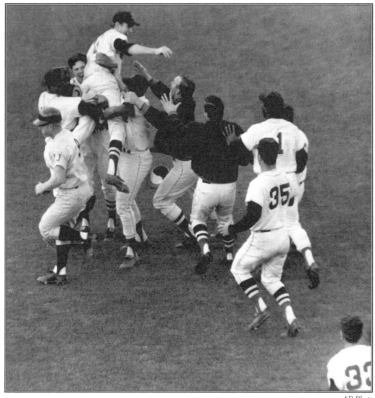

AP Photo

While the Yankees struggled in the late 1960s, the Boston Red Sox thrived. Here the team celebrates The Impossible Dream, winning the Pennant in 1967 just one year after finishing in ninth place, 26 games out. The 1967 Sox of Carl Yastrzemski and Jim Lonborg captured the hearts of New England fans and reignited a region's passion for baseball that has only grown in the nearly four decades since.

1965
THE EMPIRE CRUMBLES

The New York Yankees went to the 1964 World Series, but fell to the St. Louis Cardinals in seven games, ushering in a rapid decline to mediocrity. With the wealthy and pampered stars of the past suddenly aging, a depleted farm system, and a bigoted management that had too long resisted promoting black ballplayers, the Old Empire crumbled. After the 1964 season, the Yankees fired Yogi Berra as manager and the team was purchased by CBS. It wasn't a good investment.

In 1965, the Yankees stumbled out of the gate and never recovered, finishing sixth—their worst showing since 1925. In 1966, the remarkable collapse was complete—Mickey Mantle's Yankees finished in last place for the first time since 1912, 26.5 games out of first. The team followed its disastrous 1966 campaign with a ninth-place finish in the 10-team league in 1967.

If falling to the bottom of the league standings wasn't enough, the team had the added insult of watching the rival Red Sox win the American League pennant with their "Impossible Dream" team of 1967. The Sox—a moribund franchise throughout the 1960s following the retirement of Ted Williams—had

AP Photo

Tom Seaver of the New York Mets throws a pitch in the 1969 World Series. The Miracle Mets beat the Baltimore Orioles 4 games to 1 to win the World Series. The upstart Mets suddenly owned New York, and the Yankees were also-rans.

finished 26 games out in 1966, but powered by league MVP Carl "Yaz" Yastrzemski, who won the last Triple Crown in the Majors that year, and Cy Young Award winner Jim Lonborg, the team put it all together in 1967. That Boston Red Sox team captured the hearts of all of New England, which eventually would become known as Red Sox Nation, and reignited a regional passion for the Red Sox that has only strengthened in the twenty-first century.

Two years later, the medicine was just as bitter. The cross-town New York Mets, led by Tom Seaver's 25 wins, took New York and the nation by storm with their "Miracle Mets" season, winning the pennant and then the 1969 World Series in just their eighth season of existence. Not only were the Yankees no longer the number-one team in the Major Leagues or the American League—they weren't even the top team in New York. While the Mets were winning, the Yankees finished 28.5 games behind the Baltimore Orioles in the new American League East.

Collectively from 1965 to 1969, the Yankees finished a total 120 games out of first place. With the money spigot turned off and the old Yankee stars gone, the Yankee dynasty crumbled. Mickey Mantle finally retired, two years too late, after a 1968 season when his numbers fell to a .237 average, 18 homers, 54

1967 American League Standings

TEAM	W	L	T	GB
Boston	92	70	0	—
Minnesota	91	71	2	1
Detroit	91	71	1	1
Chicago	89	73	0	3
California	84	77	0	7.5
Washington	76	85	0	15.5
Baltimore	76	85	0	15.5
Cleveland	75	87	0	17
New York	72	90	1	20
Kansas City	62	99	0	29.5

RBIs and 97 strikeouts in 435 at bats. It was also closing time for Whitey "Slick" Ford, Mantle's longtime drinking buddy, who retired following the 1967 season (and a 2–4 record). Roger Maris, who was treated horribly by the Yankees and Yankee fans (he was the frequent target of boos), was traded to the Cardinals, where he would win another World Series. While some new players were good, they didn't have the stuff of teams in years past.

BY THE LATE '60S, THE TRADITIONALLY FRONT-RUNNING YANKEE FANS HAD ABANDONED THE TEAM. ATTENDANCE WAS BARELY REACHING 1 MILLION A YEAR, LESS THAN HALF THE NUMBERS OF 20 YEARS EARLIER. AND ON ONE STUNNING DAY IN 1966, ONLY 413 FANS SHOWED UP AT YANKEE STADIUM FOR A GAME—413!

By the late '60s, the traditionally front-running Yankee fans had abandoned the team. Attendance was barely reaching one million a year, less than half the numbers of 20 years earlier. And on one stunning day in 1966, only 413 fans showed up at Yankee Stadium for a game—413!

1982–1992
A DECADE OF HIGH-PRICED MEDIOCRITY

The span from 1982 to 1992 was marked by middling teams, a meddling owner, a revolving door of managers, and teams that were going nowhere. Sure, the Yankees opened up the purse strings again in the late 1970s to buy some more championships as a new owner reignited the big-spending, greed-oriented Yankee tradition. But hubris and folly brought the team back to earth again quickly.

In those years, five Yankee teams finished below .500. There were a dozen managerial changes. Players came and went with regularity, and the team one year used 50 different players. Between 1990–92, the team finished a collective 61.5 games out of first.

Again, the low points were made even lower by the success of rivals. In the mid-1980s, the New York Mets had the bigger stars and the better team. In 1986, the Mets won 108 regular season games and the World Series. The team from Queens came to dominate the back pages of the New York tabloids, relegating the Bronx Bombers to also-ran status and driving owner George Steinbrenner crazy.

1990 American League East Standings

Team	W	L	GB
Boston	88	74	—
Toronto	86	76	2
Detroit	79	83	9
Cleveland	77	85	11
Baltimore	76	85	11.5
Milwaukee	74	88	14
New York	67	95	21

Four years later in 1990, the fabled Yankees finished 67–95, dead last in the American League East, 21 games behind the division-winning Boston Red Sox, a team that had won three division titles in five years. In 1990, the Yankee pitching staff had the third-worst worst ERA in the 14-team American League. Meanwhile, Yankee hitters were the worst in the Majors, with league lows in average (.241), doubles and triples.

Steinbrenner seemed to make the news more than his team did with his free agent signings, ill-advised trades, boorish behavior, and suspensions. In the darkest of these years, "Steinbrenner Must Go" signs began appearing at Yankee Stadium, and "Steinbrenner Sucks" chants became endearing crowd favorites.

"WALL STREET BANKERS SUPPOSEDLY BACK THE
YANKEES; SMITH COLLEGE GIRLS APPROVE OF THEM.
GOD, BROOKS BROTHERS, AND UNITED STATES STEEL
ARE BELIEVED TO BE SOLIDLY IN THE YANKEES' CORNER
. . . THE EFFICIENTLY TRIUMPHANT YANKEE MACHINE IS
A GREAT INSTITUTION, BUT, AS THEY SAY, WHO CAN FALL
IN LOVE WITH U.S. STEEL?"

GAY TALESE
IN "THERE ARE FANS—AND YANKEE FANS"

NOW BATTING . . .

KEVIN WITT

The package came with good intentions, but the gift was presumptuous to the point it legitimately pissed me off.

Gretchen was eight months pregnant last fall. They gave her a surprise baby shower at work. She was excited later at home as she put each gift on its own pedestal.

A bag of diapers here. A gift card there. Washcloths and one-sies. Blankets and wipes.

"That's great, honey," or some derivation of that, I said each time, in between microwaving some pork chops. Then she opened a box and pulled out a blue-and-white baby Yankees outfit.

"That's nice, isn't it?" Gretchen asked.

Silence.

Madison hadn't even taken her first breath, and somebody already decided she would be a Yankees fan. They figured, why wouldn't she want to join almost everybody else in New York on that bandwagon?

"The only way my little girl is wearing that outfit," I said, "is if we run out of diapers."

Back when Daddy was just a few years out of his own diapers in the mid-1970s, he started rooting for New York's other team. The one that didn't buy Reggie and Catfish in 1977, or the Goose a year later.

As the Yankees won World Championships, the Mets fielded some of the worst teams in their history. Don't think that didn't get shoved down my throat on a regular basis.

Burger King even issued a Yankees baseball card set. My team was so bad I was lucky Topps included it.

In a neighborhood filled with right-handed Wiffle ball pitchers, everybody turned around and hit left-handed. We all wore those plastic batting helmets. The kids wearing the Yankees helmet could be Mr. October, with the big swing and the deep knee bend. I got to be Richie Hebner, who did this cool thing where he pulled at the back of his shirt collar when he stepped into the box, then slapped one to left.

I'll give those kids credit, though. None of them would have been caught dead in a lime-green Yankees cap or a T-shirt with "Ruth" printed above the number 3 across the back. This is the wardrobe of the new breed of Yankees fan, the worst of three derivations.

"THE ONLY WAY MY LITTLE GIRL IS WEARING THAT [YANKEES] OUTFIT IS IF WE RUN OUT OF DIAPERS."

The first derivation is the "I'm 72-and-rooting-for-60-years" Yankees fan, who wants to incorporate Joe D. and The Mick into every baseball discussion, thinks everybody is overpaid and loves the phrase "True Yankee."

Then there's the "Boston Sucks" Yankees fan of my generation who feels most entitled to drop the "26 World Championships" on you because they were around for all of six of them.

Each of these two types of fans thought the Scooter was a better announcer than Vin Scully, but at least they paid some dues. One rooted for Horace Clarke at second base, the other for Steve Sax. Those are battle scars.

The current lot of Yankees fans—those of the new millenium—is the sorriest of all.

He's the guy with sadness in his voice when he talks of how his four-year-old son has never seen his team win a World Championship.

She's the woman who thinks Tino Martinez is the greatest first baseman in team history. It's useless to point out that, counting coaches, he's not even the best first baseman in his own dugout.

He's the guy who had talk radio stations on speed dial last summer, and who's ticked off the Diamondbacks didn't just hand over Randy Johnson for three boxes of balls and a 12-pack.

She's the woman who expected her Yankees, with A-Rod now on board, to go get that Nomar guy to come play second. He'll change positions to come here. A-Rod did.

He's the guy who, when Roger Clemens took the money—and not King George's—turned on Clemens quicker than Henry Hill.

And she's the woman who showed up at a baby shower, ready to give Madison Witt a baseball team. Her baseball team. Everybody's baseball team.

Thanks, but no thanks. Madison isn't interested.

Kevin Witt grew up in Middletown, New York, a devoted New York Mets fan. His favorite player was Dave Kingman. Madison will soon get her first jersey—a white one with "Martinez" on the back. Kevin writes for the Times Herald-Record *of Middletown.*

THIRD INNING

Previous page—With his baseball skills diminishing in the mid-1930s, the great Babe Ruth (center, in March 1935, with Charley Dressen, left, and Bill McKechnie, right) was simply cast aside by the New York Yankees. He finished his career with the old Boston Braves of the National League, back in the city where his greatness began. After his retirement that year, it was said Ruth waited by the telephone hoping for a chance to manage that never came. The ungrateful Yankees didn't even honor Ruth on the field until 1947—twelve years after the greatest baseball player ever retired.

MONEY FOR NOTHING, DISRESPECT FOR FREE

The Yankees have a long, colorful history when it comes to hiring, firing, and trading players. They've been known to give away frightening amounts of money to over-the-hill, nonproductive, and bad players. Yet in the old days, when players had few rights, ownership was sometimes nasty, hoarding money from valuable team members and asking stars to take pay cuts following career years. The Yankees have traded away future stars and taken on players with heavy baggage. Remember, this is the team that acquired Jose Contreras, Luis Polonia and Kevin Brown, to name but a few high-priced or embarrassing busts.

The Yankees even managed to dump Babe Ruth at the end of his career—the one player perhaps single-handedly responsible for any success the Yankees have enjoyed over the years. Looking back, it seems an almost unimaginable act of disrespect. As the Babe reached the end of his career, he simply wanted a chance to manage. The Yankees discarded him. And so it was that the Babe finished out his career in Boston, back in the city where it all began, this time as a member of the old Boston Braves of the National League. Ahhh, ya gotta love that corporate Yankees machine. Just watch your back.

1985
ED WHITSON

The era of free agency convinced Yankee owner George Steinbrenner that he could buy himself a championship by seducing players with cold hard cash. And who could blame him? For the Yankees, the Gordon Gekko "Greed is Good" blueprint has been successful since the 1920s when the team bought its first World Series.

Catfish Hunter, Reggie Jackson, and Goose Gossage often come up among the names of successful Steinbrenner-era mercenaries lured by Yankee cash. And they did help the Yankees buy a World Series title or two.

But, there have been many other players, bad players, who were grossly overpaid. The worst of the lot for the Yankees may have been Ed Whitson, who was booed out of town for not living up to his expensive price tag.

Who knows what George Steinbrenner was thinking when he signed Whitson to a five-year, $4.25-million contract after the righthander had posted a 14–8 record in 1984 with the San Diego Padres. Steinbrenner certainly couldn't have been looking at Whitson's career numbers; Whitson had already played for four teams in eight years, was just 53–56 lifetime, and only twice had hit double digits in a season for win totals.

Starting off the season at 1–6, Whitson drew the boos of unmerciful Yankee fans. He made headlines in September when he broke manager Billy Martin's arm in an early morning fight in the team's hotel bar in Baltimore, suffering a broken rib and busted lip himself.

The taunts grew worse the following year. Whitson took to wearing a jacket in pregame drills to hide his uniform number, and took a long underground tunnel to the bullpen to avoid fans' taunting.

He became such a target of fan abuse that manager Lou Piniella refused to pitch him in Yankee Stadium, instead using him exclusively on the road. His ERA ballooned to 7.54, and he gave up 54 hits in just 37 innings.

The Yankees finally put Whitson out of his misery by trading him back to the Padres, where he spent the final six years of his career.

1996
KENNY ROGERS

Kenny Rogers was an acclaimed lefty who put up good numbers—not to mention a perfect game in 1994—during his years as a Texas Ranger. When George Steinbrenner opened his fat wallet and offered Rogers a four-year, $20-million contract, Rogers couldn't turn him down. But Rogers's two years in the Bronx were not the stuff of legend.

Rogers's first Yankee season was mediocre enough, with a 12–8 record and a 4.68 ERA. But it was his 1996 postseason performance, when he had an ERA of 14.14, that put him in Steinbrenner's doghouse. During the 1996 World Series against the Atlanta Braves, Rogers was telling reporters how confident he was when Steinbrenner came up, poked him in the shoulder and said, "I've heard it before. This time I want to see it."

Steinbrenner was desperate to unload Rogers after the pitcher wilted again under pressure during his 1997 season, finishing with a 6–7 record and a 5.65 ERA. Rogers ended up being traded to Oakland for a player to be named later.

1988
JAY BUHNER

In a *Seinfeld* episode, Frank Costanza yells to George Steinbrenner: "How in the hell could you trade Buhner?"

A good question. The 1988 trade of Jay Buhner and two minor league pitchers to Seattle for designated hitter Ken Phelps ranks among the stupidest trades in Yankee history.

After the trade, Buhner went on to play 14 years with Seattle, where he hit 307 homers and drove in 949 runs. He hit more than 40 home runs in three straight seasons from 1995–97—the first big leaguer to accomplish that feat since Frank Howard did it with Washington from 1968–70.

His booming bat and bald head made him a fan favorite on a star-laden Mariners team—and a cause for frustration among Yankee fans (Frank Costanza among them).

The lumbering Phelps was a bust, playing just 131 games for the Yankees in parts of two seasons, managing 17 homers and 51 RBIs. He was unloaded in August 1989, when the team sent him to Oakland for pitcher Scott Holcom.

The following season, the A's sold Phelps to the Cleveland Indians, where he went 7-for-61 with no homers or RBIs to finish out the season—and his career.

1998
MIKE LOWELL FOR THREE MINOR LEAGUERS

In 1998, New York's front office decided to trade prospect and one-time Minor League Player of the Year Mike Lowell for three minor league pitchers in the Florida Marlins' organization.

Lowell went on to become an everyday third baseman with power. In his first five seasons as a regular through 2004, he was averaging about 25 homers and nearly 100 RBIs a season.

In fact, he's already earned a place in the Hall of Fame. The bat he used to hit a grand slam on August 9, 1999, a record fifth slam around the Majors that day, is on display in Cooperstown.

In return for Lowell, the Yankees received pitchers Eddie Yarnall, Todd Noel, and Mark Johnson. Yarnall pitched a total of just 20 innings for the Yankees in 1999 and 2000, winning one game in the process. Noel and Johnson never threw a single pitch for the club.

1942
TOMMY HOLMES FOR MOORE AND HASSETT

Outfielder Tommy Holmes could have been a great Yankee—if the team hadn't traded him away to the Boston Braves in 1942.

In return for Holmes, the Braves gave up Gene Moore and Buddy Hassett. Hassett played one season for the Yankees and then joined the navy and didn't make it back to the Major Leagues. Moore never played a game for the Yankees; the team shipped him off in another trade just three weeks after obtaining him.

Holmes, however, went on to play 10 years for the Braves, ending his career with a .302 average. In 1945, he was the league leader in hits (224), doubles (47), home runs (28) and slugging percentage (.577). He was second in batting average and RBIs and third in runs scored. To this day, he is the only player to ever lead the league in home runs while having the fewest strikeouts (9).

Also in 1945, Holmes set a National League record with a 37-game hitting streak, a record that stood until 1978.

1918
URBAN SHOCKER FOR PRATT AND PLANK

Urban Shocker was a spot starter for the Yankees when he and three position players were traded to the St. Louis Browns before the start of the 1918 season. In return, New York got second baseman Del Pratt and pitcher Eddie Plank.

Plank, who must have been a smart, decent guy, refused to report to the Yankees and retired. Pratt had three decent seasons for the club, hitting .314 in 1920. But the Browns clearly got the best of this deal, with Shocker—a righthander known for his spitball and other junk pitches—being the key.

Following the trade, Shocker won 126 games for the Browns. He won more than 20 games for four straight years, from 1920–23, topping out in 1921 with a 27–12 record.

It's been speculated that had the Yankees had Shocker, they might have secured pennants in 1920, when they finished three games out, and in 1924 when the team came in second by two games. Manager Miller Huggins later remarked that shipping Shocker to the Browns was one of the worst trades he ever made.

The Browns traded Shocker back to New York in 1925, where he ended up his career before dying in 1928 of an enlarged heart, which had given him dizzy spells and shortness of breath and forced him to sleep sitting up much of the time.

1935
NO WAY TO TREAT A HERO

There is no doubt that Babe Ruth made the Yankees what they were in the 1920s and 1930s, and set them up for all future success as well. The Sultan of Swat transformed baseball, and was such an enormous draw that he alone established the Yankees as a household name, drawing so many fans that Yankees revenue dwarfed that of their competition. Yet when his skills started to diminish with age, the Yankees showed their appreciation as only the Yankees could—they kicked him out the door. He was released in 1935.

Ruth had always expressed an interest in managing the Yankees, but the bloodless team officials had no intention of allowing that to happen. Team owner Jacob Ruppert is said to have told Ruth: "Manage the Yankees? You can't even manage yourself!" So they released him.

Then, it was the Yankees who acted as if they held a grudge. First, club officials had the audacity to give Ruth's number 3 jersey to his replacement, George Selkirk (who as a result was booed mercilessly by fans his first few games). And then when the team began retiring numbers, it wasn't Ruth's that was retired first—but Lou Gehrig's. The team had seemingly put Ruth out to pasture and forgotten he was there.

After leaving the Yankees, Ruth signed with the old Boston Braves of the National League as a player and assistant manager, hoping to use his time there as a catalyst to a managerial post. Ironically, he was back in the city where it all started.

Ruth's career began with the Boston Red Sox in 1914. He played six seasons at Fenway Park and helped the team win three World Championships. His all-around talent was staggering. While in Boston, he posted an 89–46 record as a pitcher, and as a batter he hit .308, with 49 homers and 230 RBIs.

His last hurrah came on May 25, 1935, at old Forbes Field in Pittsburgh when he hit three homers in a single game, including his record 714th. However, it quickly became clear that the Braves were more interested in using Ruth as a drawing card than in making him a manager. A week after his three-homer performance, he quit. In all, Ruth played in 28 games for the Braves in 1935, hitting .181 with six home runs and 12 RBI. It is said that for the rest of his life, he sat by the telephone waiting for a call to manage that never came.

It certainly didn't come from the Yankees. In fact, the Yankees didn't bother honoring him until 1947—12 years after he officially retired. Babe Ruth Day on April 27, 1947, featured speeches and gifts, but the team still didn't go to the trouble of retiring his jersey number; that didn't happen until the following year—10 years after Lou Gehrig's number was retired. At that ceremony, an ailing Ruth spoke with a raspy voice. And just two months later, on August 16, 1948, Babe Ruth, the greatest baseball player of all time, was dead, from throat cancer. He was only 53.

"REGGIE JACKSON COULDN'T SHINE WILLIE MAYS'S SHOES. HE NEVER HIT .300, HE'S A BUTCHER IN THE OUTFIELD AND HE'S GOT A BIG MOUTH. WHAT DOES HE MAKE, $8,000 A WEEK? I WOULDN'T PAY HIM $8 A WEEK. HE'S A BUM."

LEO DUROCHER,
FORMER MAJOR LEAGUE MANAGER

NOW BATTING . . .

JOHN HOLYOKE

Contrary to popular opinion, we Yankee haters aren't *born* that way. Nope. No way. As babies, we simply don't possess enough bile and venom. As toddlers, we simply don't know enough about the world to form such a reasoned opinion.

Eventually, however—if we were lucky enough to grow up in Red Sox Nation—we *learn* to hate, in that more-or-less good-natured way that more-or-less good-natured sports fans hate. We evolve (or get beaten down, if you prefer) only after years of frustration and disappointment finally take their toll.

We sit. We watch. We learn. We cry. And then, eventually, we hate.

We learn that the Red Sox are the good guys, and that the Yankees are the kind of cocky miscreants who get candy bars named after them. We learn that for every nearly likeable Yankee like Ron Guidry or Thurman Munson, there is a Reggie Jackson.

And we learn that even if a roster full of Boy Scouts dons pinstripes in a given year (it hasn't happened yet, but I suppose it could), there is always a man named Steinbrenner pulling the strings . . . and he's clearly worthy of all of the hatred we can muster.

In some ways, I figure, it's easiest to hate what you don't know. And I simply don't know the Yankees. Not really. I've never met a Yankee, never written a story about one, and have never even seen them play baseball in person.

All I know about the Yankees is what I have read, what I have listened to on car radios, and what I have seen replayed over and over on TV. Many of my fellow Mainers are like me in that regard—the Yankees are bad; *evil*, even. We accept this, even if we've not been fortunate enough to actually sit in the stands at Fenway on a steamy July evening and add our voices to the chorus of cat-calls directed at real, actual Yankees.

AND WE LEARN THAT EVEN IF A ROSTER FULL OF BOY SCOUTS DONS PINSTRIPES IN A GIVEN YEAR (IT HASN'T HAPPENED YET, BUT I SUPPOSE IT COULD), THERE IS ALWAYS A MAN NAMED STEINBRENNER PULLING THE STRINGS . . . AND HE'S CLEARLY WORTHY OF ALL THE HATRED WE CAN MUSTER.

Eventually, of course, our dislike of the Yanks becomes more than that. Something happens. Something bad. Something life-changing. Something personal . . . something like a special-delivery, take-that Hallmark greeting intended solely for us.

For me, that greeting arrived on my fourteenth birthday. Up until then, I loved the Sox, tolerated everyone else (even the Yankees), and knew that no matter what happened, next year was *the* year.

On October 2, 1978, I turned fourteen. Sidelined from Pop Warner football because of a broken arm, I dutifully pedaled to practice every day anyway. That day, I carried a small transistor radio so I could keep my teammates updated on the biggest game of the year. The Sox had collapsed as the regular season of '78 wound down, but that didn't matter. All it took was one win over the Yankees—a perfect birthday present, I figured—in the winner-take-all playoff, and everything would be forgiven.

You know the rest. Mike Torrez pitching with a lead. Light-hitting Bucky Dent at the plate. A pop fly into the Boston sky.

A home run that cemented my own evolution.

A home run that I still don't believe.

And a home run that I still can't forgive. Even after the 2004 World Championship. Even if the Sox win the next five.

That's the way we Yankee haters are, you see. No matter what happens, we've always recognized the inherent value of a good, old-fashioned grudge.

John Holyoke is a columnist for the Bangor Daily News. *He grew up in Brewer, Maine, and graduated from the University of Maine in 1993. He began working at the News as a sports clerk, and became a full-time columnist in 2003.*

Fourth Inning

AP Photo

Previous page—Marilyn Monroe and Joe DiMaggio on January 29, 1954, about two weeks after their wedding. The storybook marriage of the baseball hero and the Hollywood goddess was anything but a fairy tale. Among other things, the Yankee Clipper, jealous of Monroe's fame and attention, beat her during their short-lived marriage. Monroe filed for divorce less than one year after they were married.

BAD BOYS, BAD BOYS

The Yankees love to have their players portray a squeaky-clean, spit-and-shine image—the type that reflects well upon the team's corporate mentality. It is part of their myth-and-awe campaign, long aided and abetted by the Yankee Amen Chorus, also known as the New York media. Despite fawning news reporting and Yankee corporate spin over the years, the true nature of some players has eventually leaked out. (And in recent years, the leak has been more like a flood, except, perhaps, for golden boys like Derek Jeter.)

Off-field drinking, drugs, and bad behavior have been as much a staple of Yankee players as unchecked egos. It started early in the franchise's history and continues to this day. Certainly such behavior runs contrary to the Yankee myth that they won't put up with bad behavior from players. Well, yes they will, so long as they can play.

There are so many Bad Boy Yankees you could write a book—or two or three or four or five—about them. Each of them has his own story, but they all have one thing in common: They bring embarrassment to the Yankees. In no particular order, here are some of the true lowlights in Yankee behavior.

The son of a Baltimore saloonkeeper, Babe Ruth was stealing, chewing tobacco, cussing, and refusing to go to school by age seven. He was declared "incorrigible," and his parents shipped him off to a reformatory where he spent most of his years until he was 18.

During his baseball career, he was just as hopeless. When he made the big leagues, he was loud and obnoxious with a gargantuan appetite for food, booze, willing women, and life in the fast lane.

As baseball's greatest superstar, Ruth made more money—and spent more money—than anybody around. He sipped bourbon and ginger ale before breakfast and was a regular at whorehouses around the country. He tucked his wife and adopted daughter away at a rural Massachusetts farmhouse while he kept a suite on New York's Upper West Side and drove a Packard with his initials monogrammed on the driver's-side door.

His passion for the fast life was matched by his dislike for authority. He once defied the baseball commissioner, Mountain Landis, by going on a barnstorming tour following the 1921 season, and told Landis to jump in a lake. In response, Landis suspended and fined Ruth.

The following season Ruth was suspended for throwing dirt in an umpire's face and then climbing into the stands to go after a heckler. When fans booed, he stood atop the dugout and shook his fist and yelled.

In 1925, he showed up to the spring season overweight and often drunk, torn between his estranged wife and another woman. When he collapsed with an illness that hospitalized him for seven weeks, reporters privately speculated that he had venereal disease, but they publicly wrote that he had eaten too many hot dogs and drank too many sodas. His manager fined him $5,000—more than many players were making in a season.

Ruth lit up half-smoked cigars he found on men's room floors. It's been reported he once ate an 18-egg omelet, and that

Ty Cobb saw him eat half a dozen sandwiches and a jar of pig knuckles and then wash that down with a pitcher of beer. It's also been said that when the Yankees played in Chicago, Ruth drank beer between innings at a bar called McCuddy's across from Comiskey Park.

MICKEY MANTLE
HANGOVER HOME RUNS

Mickey Mantle reckoned that playing with a hangover was simply a part of baseball. He once admitted that he sometimes saw three balls heading toward home plate and simply swung at the middle one. It was all very contrary to the clean-cut and innocent Mantle image spoon-fed to the public by the Yankees and the media.

Mantle disregarded training programs and even failed his physical in 1953. Mantle, Billy Martin, and Whitey Ford were an inseparable trio, often staying out all night drinking and carousing. Mantle basically never grew up. Like an adolescent with raging hormones, he used mirrors to peek under the doors of hotel rooms when he was on road trips, and he would lead a group of players to hotel rooftops so they could peep through windows at women undressing.

While the public image of Mantle often shows a smiling, happy-go-lucky guy, he was portrayed as an often mean-hearted drunk in *Ball Four*, the landmark baseball book by Jim Bouton that helped lift the veil of secrecy from baseball players and exposed their often flawed behavior. In the book, which infuriated the Yankees, Bouton wrote that Mantle would push aside or slam windows on little kids seeking his autograph. Only after his career ended did the world learn of Mantle's heavy drinking, womanizing, abusiveness, and otherwise reckless behavior.

At his retirement, at age 37, Mantle cracked: "If I'd known I was going to last this long, I would have taken better care of myself when I was younger."

For Mantle, alcohol was as much a part of his life as baseball. In *Mickey Mantle: America's Prodigal Son*, author Tony Castro wrote that Mantle found it the macho thing to do to be "the Man" off the field as well as on it, proving his manliness by how much he could drink, how many women he could bed, and how late he could stay up.

AT AN EXCLUSIVE COUNTRY CLUB IN DALLAS WHERE HE BELONGED, MANTLE USED TO SURPRISE MEMBERS BY SKINNY-DIPPING IN THE POOL AND WALKING INTO THE RESTAURANT NAKED TO ORDER A DRINK. THE CLUB HAD TO INSTITUTE THE "MICKEY MANTLE RULE," PROHIBITING ANYONE FROM ENTERING THE CLUB'S RESTAURANT IN THE NUDE.

He embarrassed and emotionally abused his wife with his behavior, publicly humiliating her over and over again. In retirement, his drinking worsened. He was known to drink the "breakfast of champions" (Kahlua, brandy and cream) in the morning, four or five glasses of wine over lunch and vodka at dinner. At an exclusive country club in Dallas where he belonged, Mantle used to surprise members by skinny-dipping in the pool and walking into the restaurant naked to order a drink. The club had to institute the "Mickey Mantle Rule," prohibiting anyone from entering the club's restaurant in the nude.

All that fast living eventually caught up with Mantle. He was treated for alcoholism, but his damaged liver was ravaged by cirrhosis, hepatitis C, and cancer that led to his death in 1995. He was 63.

HAL CHASE
THE GAMBLING PRINCE

Hal Chase had a fair bat and a terrific glove during his nine-year career with the Yankees from 1905–1913. But his dark reputation of consorting with gamblers and throwing games makes him of more interest to criminologists than to baseball fans. Some say he was baseball's all-time biggest crook.

Charming, handsome and skilled, Chase came to be known as "Prince Hal." But he was so bold in his association with known gamblers that fans sometimes chanted "What's the odds?" when he took the field.

While Chase played for the Yankees, managers George Stallings and later Frank Chance accused him of fixing games. League and team officials wouldn't do anything, however, because Chase was one of the bigger drawing cards for the team and the league (Perhaps an early sign of Yankee favoritism by Major League Baseball).

When Chase later played for Cincinnati, it was manager Christy Mathewson who suspected him of throwing games by making errant throws to first when the pitcher covered. When Chase later landed with the New York Giants, manager John McGraw had the same suspicions.

After conclusive proof of Chase's gambling was put forth, Chase and two other big league players were quietly blackballed out of the National League in 1919. Chase's name has been repeatedly linked to the 1919 Black Sox scandal, when the Chicago White Sox threw the World Series. Testimony revealed that Chase won nearly $40,000 betting against the White Sox in the 1919 World Series, and that he may have had a hand in working with gamblers who paid off the players.

In his later years, he was implicated in a gambling ring that pervaded the Pacific Coast League. So much for reform.

RUBEN RIVERA
THOU SHALT NOT STEAL

Ruben Rivera was released by the Yankees in spring training of 2002 after he stole Derek Jeter's glove and bat and sold them to a memorabilia dealer for $2,500.

The Yankees settled Rivera's $1-million contract for $200,000. Rivera told a TV station in his native Panama that he was surprised he was cut, saying other players have gotten breaks for drug use and other infractions.

"Everyone makes mistakes," said Rivera, who was later picked up by Texas, where he hit .209. "I haven't killed anybody. It was a moment when I wasn't thinking right."

MIKE KEKICH AND FRITZ PETERSON
MIKE AND MARILYN AND FRITZ AND SUZANNE

Mike Kekich and Fritz Peterson, a pair of lefty pitchers, shocked the Yankees in 1973 with the news that they had swapped families.

When they arrived at spring training that year, they announced they had traded spouses, children, houses, cars, and even the family dogs. They insisted they were "life-swapping," not "wife-swapping."

Even in the wacky 1970s, just four years after the movie *Bob & Carol & Ted & Alice*, their move was more than a bit eccentric. It was downright anti-Yankee. Team general manager Lee MacPhail was heard to quip: "We may have to call off Family Day."

Mike Kekich and Marilyn Peterson ended their relationship three months later. But Suzanne Kekich and Fritz Peterson married the following year and eventually had four children together.

The Yankees, seeking to defuse an embarrassing situation, quickly shipped Kekich off to Cleveland, where he lasted a year. Peterson was sent to the Indians in early 1974 for Chris Chambliss, where he lasted three years before retiring.

Peterson is tenth all-time for innings pitched for the Yankees, fourteenth in wins, fourteenth in strikeouts and thirteenth in shutouts.

JOE DiMAGGIO
A JOLTIN' EGO

Joltin' Joe DiMaggio attracted almost no criticism during his 13-year career with the Yankees. He was successfully promoted as the best all-around player of his time, idolized by fans, teammates, opponents, and reporters.

But the relationship was one-sided and a distortion of reality. DiMaggio was self-centered, greedy, manipulative, bitter, paranoid and jealous, and a wife-beater. He was the antithesis of the larger-than-life Babe Ruth, who loved the crowds and their adulation. DiMaggio took meals in his hotel room, ignoring his worshipping fans.

In the book *Joe DiMaggio: The Hero's Life*, author Richard Ben Cramer wrote that DiMaggio hung out with mobsters, figuring they were always good for a broad or a night out on the town. He was obsessed with money, and so cheap that he spent only six and a half bucks on a motel room on his wedding night with Marilyn Monroe.

He was estranged from his brothers and his son, Joe Jr. When he sold out his share of the "Joe DiMaggio's Grotto" restaurant in San Francisco to other family members, he insisted that the name "Joe" be taken off the sign. When his brother

Dom, a former center fielder with the Boston Red Sox, asked him to write the foreword to his book, Joe asked to be paid.

DiMaggio was estranged from his teammates, too. None of them could honestly call him a friend. He and Mantle had a chilly relationship that lasted until the end of their lives. On Mickey Mantle Day in 1995, DiMaggio seethed when the Mickey Mantle Commemorative Day baseball was issued. Collectors immediately drove up the price to $300 a ball, and DiMaggio, in true Joe DiMaggio fashion, was incensed that Mantle balls were fetching double what his balls were going for—and his were autographed. After his retirement, DiMaggio always insisted that he be introduced in public as "Baseball's Greatest Living Ballplayer."

Despite everything, DiMaggio's public persona rarely took a hit during his playing days, not even after Marilyn Monroe divorced him after he beat her, nor after he became a huckster for Mr. Coffee. In DiMaggio's case, his standoffishness was mistaken for class, and his icon status served as a protective facade for a very troubled man.

BILLY MARTIN
BARROOM BRAWLER

The son of a philandering truck driver and a sometime prostitute, Billy Martin was a raucous, hard-drinking brawler during his Major League career from 1950 to 1961.

Although his statistics weren't much to brag about, he was known as a clutch player with a feisty spirit who did what it took to win.

But it was that spirit, along with spirits of the drinking kind, that got him in trouble. He had numerous fights with opposing players, teammates, fans, and critics, and once popped Red Sox outfielder Jimmy Piersall twice in the face under the stands in Boston.

Martin never backed down from an opponent on the ball field, and the same was true in a saloon. After a barroom incident at the Copacabana in New York in 1957, Yankees general manager George Weiss—believing Martin to be very un-Yankee-like—traded him to Kansas City.

Martin retired as a player in 1961 after playing out his final six years with six different teams. But his Yankee career was far from over, and he returned as manager—again and again and again. And the barroom fights continued—again and again and again—in Anaheim, in Baltimore, in Texas and wherever else the team played. A tanked-up Martin once punched out a marshmallow salesman at a hotel bar in Bloomington, Minnesota.

Martin was first hired as Yankee manager in 1975 and lasted until 1978, with two league championships and a World Series title to his credit. Owner George Steinbrenner brought him back four more times.

Martin got fired the first time after talking to reporters at Chicago's O'Hare Airport. After several drinks—when else?—he said, "The two of them deserve each other. One's a born liar, the other's convicted." He was referring to Reggie Jackson as a liar, and Steinbrenner as being convicted, for illegal campaign contributions to Richard Nixon. The following day Martin tearfully resigned.

Martin was back managing for Steinbrenner the following year, but was fired for a second time after getting into a fistfight with the marshmallow salesman that October. After managing the Oakland A's for a couple of years, he was rehired to manage the Yankees for all of 1983, for most of 1985, and for about half of 1988. Following the end of his managerial career, Steinbrenner hired him again, this time as a special consultant.

Martin died on Christmas Day 1989 in a single-vehicle accident near his home in New York State. He was 61.

JOE PEPITONE
REBEL WITHOUT A CAUSE

Fun-loving and carefree, Joe Pepitone was a Brooklyn kid who was sometimes called a rebel without a cause. Although blessed with God-given talent, he had a nose for trouble that left him with a legacy of underachievement and overindulgence.

As a 17-year-old fresh out of high school, he blew his $20,000 signing bonus on a boat and a car. Three years later he was in a Yankees uniform as a backup to first baseman Bill Skowron. Some old buddies from Brooklyn offered to break Skowron's legs so Pepitone could be the starting first baseman, but he turned down the offer. He eventually became the starter in 1963 and remained with the team through the 1969 season, earning three Gold Gloves and hitting 166 home runs.

REPORTS SAID THAT POLICE FOUND A BLOODIED AND DISORIENTED PEPITONE WALKING THROUGH THE TUNNEL AND MUMBLING, "I'M JOE PEPITONE, I'M JOE PEPITONE, I'M JOE PEPITONE."

But Pepitone is better remembered for his off-field activities. He frequented late-night haunts, was on the constant prowl for loose women, picked up cheap hookers, and was often hounded by ex-wives and loan sharks. He was a nonconformist and didn't care what others thought of him. His teammates were appalled when he brought a hair dryer with him on road trips. While with the Chicago Cubs later in his career, he wore love beads and psychedelic clothing.

After leaving the Yankees three times in 1969, he was traded to the Astros and later played with the Cubs and Braves before going to play in Japan in 1973. There, he became the typical ugly American, wearing his hair long and griping about high prices and bad food. Sick of Japan, he left the team and the country after only 14 games, with a .163 batting average. His last name became an eponym for a player who goofs off.

In 1989, he served two months of a jail term for drug and weapons offenses before the Yankees hired him as part of a work-release program. Three years later, he was charged with assault after a scuffle at a hotel in Kiamesha Lake, New York, that started when somebody called him a has-been.

In 1998, he was charged following a drunken-driving accident in New York's Midtown Tunnel, where he drove his car off the left and right walls. Reports said that police found a bloodied and disoriented Pepitone walking through the tunnel and mumbling, "I'm Joe Pepitone, I'm Joe Pepitone, I'm Joe Pepitone."

STEVE HOWE
STRIKE SEVEN, YOU'RE OUT

Steve Howe was a flamethrower lefty with a hard fastball and a nasty appetite for cocaine that had gotten him suspended from baseball half a dozen times. He also had a history of missing team flights, showing up late for games, alcohol abuse and—well, you get the picture.

In 1991, Howe, a one-time National League Rookie of the Year, had been out of baseball for four years, but he still could throw and that's all that mattered to the Yankees. They signed him.

Surprise! Trouble continued to dog Howe. After the 1991 season, he was arrested on charges in his hometown of Kalispell, Montana, for attempting to buy a gram of cocaine. The next year he was suspended, after which he was reinstated. Same old story.

Howe was finally released by the Yankees in June of 1996, not because of his drug problems but because he'd lost his stuff—his ERA had ballooned to 6.35. Three days later, he was under arrest for carrying a loaded .357 Magnum handgun in his luggage while trying to board a plane.

For all his talent, the only record Howe set was for being suspended seven times—a record that probably will stand for a while, until another Yankee player sees fit to break it.

JASON GIAMBI
STEROID MAN

Apparently it wasn't just a workout regimen that turned Jason Giambi into a home-run hitting machine.

Giambi joined the Yankees in 2002 after hitting 81 homers and 257 RBIs with Oakland in the two previous seasons. He continued his hard hitting after putting on pinstripes, banging 41 round-trippers in each of his first two seasons as a Yankee.

But in 2004 he was sick for most of the year with an intestinal parasite and a tumor on his pituitary gland. At season's end it became public that he injected himself with human growth hormone in 2003 and used steroids for three years.

Before a federal grand jury investigating a nutritional supplement laboratory in the San Francisco area, Giambi described how he injected human growth hormone into his stomach, and testosterone into his buttocks, according to the *San Francisco Chronicle*. He also rubbed a steroid known as "the cream" onto his body and placed drops of "the clear" under his tongue.

His testimony created a ruckus in the Major Leagues and made him out to be a cheater. It also made him out to be a liar because he had previously vehemently denied ever using steroids.

When he missed more than half of the 2004 season, many people questioned if the unusual ailments were related to steroids. But even then, Giambi claimed he was clean.

DAVID WELLS
PERFECT HE AIN'T

David "Boomer" Wells was a beer-bellied, bar-hopping, motorcycle-riding outlaw with a left arm that could whip 90-plus-mile-per-hour fastballs for the Yankees.

He also had a knack for putting his foot in his mouth, as evidenced by his book, *Perfect I'm Not! Boomer on Beer, Brawls, Backaches and Baseball*. Promotional materials said the book chronicled "life inside locker rooms, hotel rooms, planes, dugouts, buses, bedrooms, restaurants, titty bars, and more." It came out during spring training of 2003, just in time to piss off Yankee executives, teammates and Major League Baseball.

In the book, Wells managed to take a few potshots at teammates, most prominently Roger Clemens. Wells also wrote that an estimated 25 to 40 percent of Major Leaguers use steroids.

He claimed that he was "half-drunk" when he pitched his perfect game against Minnesota in 1998. He recalled getting drunk at a *Saturday Night Live* cast party that ended in the early hours on the day of the game. The 15th perfect game in baseball was pitched half-drunk with "bloodshot eyes, monster breath and a raging, skull-rattling hangover," he wrote.

The Yankees fined Wells $100,000 for tarnishing the team's squeaky-clean image. Wells claimed he hadn't read the galleys that had been widely distributed to the media, and issued an apology to anybody who would listen. And he backed away from the claim that he pitched his perfect game half-drunk, saying instead that he was just hungover.

Even though Wells could throw hard and win games, the teams he played for often grew tired of his lack of conditioning, his narcissism and his mouth. During his career, teams released, traded or allowed him to leave as a free agent no fewer than nine times. So it was no surprise that at the end of 2003, the Yankees let him go.

REGGIE JACKSON
BIG BAT, BIGGER MOUTH

Reggie Jackson was an egotistical punk with a big bat and an even bigger mouth when he arrived in New York in 1977 for the start of a stormy five-year stint.

When he came to the Big Apple, he became the game's highest-paid player with his five-year, $3-million contract. Even before joining the team, he created friction with teammates with his comments about "the magnitude of me." He exacerbated the situation when he was quoted in *Sport* magazine as saying, "I'm the straw that stirs the drink; Munson could only stir it bad," a reference to Yankee clubhouse leader Thurman Munson. He then made a bad situation worse when he ignored the extended hands of teammates after hitting a home run the night the article appeared.

Less than three months into his first season with the Yankees, Jackson was pulled from a game for casually playing a bloop single. The ensuing scene—captured on national TV—showed Jackson screaming at manager Billy Martin, and Martin trying to break free from coaches holding him back to get at Jackson. That dugout fight set the tone for several years to come. With Martin, Steinbrenner, Jackson, and other team members constantly at each other's throats, the team became known as the Bronx Zoo. The reputation would follow them for the next decade.

TEAMMATE GRAIG NETTLES TRADED PUNCHES WITH JACKSON DURING A WORLD SERIES VICTORY DINNER. "THE BEST THING ABOUT BEING A YANKEE IS GETTING TO WATCH REGGIE PLAY EVERY DAY," NETTLES ONCE SAID. "OF COURSE, THE WORST THING ABOUT BEING A YANKEE IS GETTING TO WATCH REGGIE PLAY EVERY DAY."

Jackson had plenty of adoring fans, but he also had plenty of enemies. When you go around saying things like, "I am the best in baseball," you're bound to tick off a few people.

Teammate Graig Nettles traded punches with Jackson during a World Series victory dinner. "The best thing about being a Yankee is getting to watch Reggie play every day," Nettles once said. "Of course, the worst thing about being a Yankee is getting to watch Reggie play every day."

"I SQUIRM WHEN I SEE ATHLETES PRAYING BEFORE A GAME. DON'T THEY REALIZE THAT IF GOD TOOK SPORTS SERIOUSLY, HE NEVER WOULD HAVE CREATED GEORGE STEINBRENNER?"

MARK RUSSELL,
AMERICAN POLITICAL COMMENTATOR AND SATIRIST

NOW BATTING . . .

CLARKE CANFIELD

I was barely old enough to ride when I began clothespinning baseball cards to my bicycle spokes. Not just any cards, mind you—Yankee cards.

It was the mid-'60s, and I was an avid baseball card collector. I had hundreds of them that I kept in an old 6.5-gallon popcorn tin in the corner of my bedroom. The players from other teams stayed in the tin can, to be looked at and studied until I remembered every single statistic (down to pinch hits and bases on balls) from every single card.

But the Yankee cards—Mantle, Maris, Ford, Pepitone, Kubek, Richardson and the others—were given special treatment. I jammed them into my bicycle spokes and rode with the wind until the cards were torn to shreds, clickety-click by clickety-click.

My friends weren't so particular about which cards they stuck onto their spokes—any old one would do for them as long as they achieved the desired clickety-click effect. But my loathing of the Yankees reached depths they could only imagine. I was a Boston native, transplanted to the St. Louis suburbs in the mid-'60s. I recalled the headlines of merciless poundings the Red Sox endured at the hands of the Yankees. I knew the stories of the smug and cocksure Yankee dominance. Hating the Yankees was in my blood, a longtime Boston tradition, and I wasn't about to fail to do my part.

So it was only natural that when it came to spoke-jamming, the Yankees were the cards of choice for my red Schwinn three-speed. I'd ride in a flash until the clicking of the cards was so fast it became a whir like a plane's propeller. And what became of the cards? They tattered and frayed and shredded and virtually disintegrated, to my delight. If they fell off the spokes, I'd turn around and run over them, with a big old grin stretched across my face.

The years passed and Yankee players came and went. But my ill will toward the team remained constant—and became stronger once I moved back to New England as an adult. There were new sets of Yankee characters to hate: Jackson, Nettles, Dent, Jeter, Strawberry, Posada, A-Rod and former Red Sox players like Clemens and Boggs. I even hated the good guys, like Mattingly, just because they wore pinstripes. At the top of the list was Steinbrenner, a symbol of greedy arrogance.

I look back on those spoke-jamming years with fondness. I'm sure I destroyed a valuable Mickey Mantle or Roger Maris card along the way, possibly throwing away a future small fortune for the jubilation of the moment. That realization, though, just gives me one more reason to hate the Yankees.

Clarke Canfield, the author of this book, was born with a Red Sox hat on his head and a Ted Williams baseball card in his hand.

FIFTH INNING

AP Photo

Previous page—One of the most embarrassing moments in Yankee history played out on October 19 before a national audience in Game 6 of the 2004 American League Championship Series versus the Boston Red Sox. With the Yankees trailing in the eighth inning at Yankee Stadium, Alex Rodriguez hit a slow roller back to pitcher Bronson Arroyo. As both raced toward first base, Rodriguez inexplicably reached out and slapped the ball out of Arroyo's glove. He was called out for interference, helped kill a potential rally, and was jeered as classless for the act.

MEMORABLE MOMENTS

For Yankee haters, some of the most memorable Yankee moments have come not in the agony of defeat, but in episodes that bordered on the absurd. The best of these occasions spare nobody: Players, coaches, managers, team executives and fans will all go down in memory—if not history—for their ludicrousness and downright idiocy. These instances involve cheating, bad sportsmanship, pettiness, ego and other characteristics that make the Yankees who they are.

1983
THE PINE TAR GAME

With Goose Gossage pitching and the Yankees nursing a two-run lead over the Kansas City Royals on July 24, 1983, George Brett hit a two-out ninth-inning homer to give the Royals a 5–4 lead. But Yankee manager Billy Martin, now in his third go-round with the club, protested the round-tripper by accusing Brett of having pine tar on his bat handle that exceeded the 17 inches allowed in the rules.

The umps agreed and nullified the homer, giving the Yankees a 4–3 win. But saner heads prevailed and had the last laugh.

American League president Lee MacPhail upheld the Royals' protest, ordering the game replayed on August 18 at the point of

Martin's outburst with Kansas City in the lead, 5–4. Martin protested the replaying of the ninth inning in his own unique way by having pitcher Ron Guidry play outfield and lefty first baseman Don Mattingly play second base. Royals' reliever Dan Quisenberry shut down the Yankees in the ninth and the Royals won—pine tar be damned.

2004
ALEX "SLAP-HAPPY" RODRIGUEZ

The Yankees not only made history in 2004 with their unprecedented choke in blowing a three-games-to-none lead against the Boston Red Sox, but they did so in grand Yankee style.

In the eighth inning of game 6, the frustrated Yankees were losing 4–1 when Derek Jeter hit an RBI single to close the gap to two. Up came Alex Rodriguez, the highest-paid player in baseball history (who would turn in a 2 for 17 performance over the deciding four games in the biggest series of his life). A-Rod hit a tapper to pitcher Bronson Arroyo on the right side. As he came barreling down the base path, A-Rod slapped—like a schoolgirl—Arroyo's forearm, knocking the ball out of his glove and down the right-field line. Jeter scampered home and A-Rod scurried into second.

RED SOX PITCHING ACE CURT SCHILLING LATER CALLED RODRIGUEZ CLASSLESS. HE TOLD ESPN RADIO THAT THE SLAP "WAS FREAKIN' JUNIOR HIGH BASEBALL AT ITS BEST. FIRST OF ALL, BRONSON WASN'T IN THE BASELINE TO BEGIN WITH. HE COULD HAVE EASILY BROKEN HIS ARM. C'MON, THAT WAS TIRED."

Red Sox manager Terry Francona was quick to argue and the umps called Rodriguez out, ruling him guilty of interference for intentionally knocking the ball out of Arroyo's glove. Jeter was ordered back to first and the rally was stifled.

But Rodriguez and Jeter began whining about the call, prompting the Yankee fans in the stands to begin throwing baseballs, beers and other junk onto the field. Riot police were called in to keep order.

Red Sox pitching ace Curt Schilling later called Rodriguez classless. He told ESPN Radio that the slap "was freakin' junior high baseball at its best."

2000
ROGER CLEMENS: BEAN BALLS AND BEAN BATS

Game 2 of the 2000 World Series between the Yankees and their crosstown rivals, the Mets, was highly anticipated, marking the first meeting between Roger Clemens and Mike Piazza since the hard-throwing Clemens, a notorious head-hunter, beaned Piazza earlier in the season—knocking him out and giving him a concussion.

Clemens, whose career was peppered with erratic and hot-tempered behavior, insisted he was just throwing inside when his fastball hit Piazza's helmet in July. But Mets players and fans claimed he did it on purpose.

When the two faced off again in game 2 of the Subway Series, Clemens threw a 1–2 fastball that ran in on Piazza's hands. Piazza swung and fouled off the ball—shattering the bat in two in the process. The jagged head of the bat bounced toward Clemens, while Piazza retained the handle in his hands.

For some reason—it's a mystery even to this day—Clemens picked up the jagged portion of wood and hurled it toward Piazza, who was making his way down the first-base line, unsure of where the ball was.

The bat missed Piazza, but not by much, and he was clearly miffed. He walked toward Clemens, shouting "What's your problem?" Clemens eased his way behind Yankee catcher Jorge

Posada, turned to the home plate umpire and said—no joke—"I thought it was the ball."

The moment was Clemens-esque all the way—not to mention stupid. How, after all, can somebody confuse a round white baseball with a jagged, shattered end of a bat? And why would you throw "the ball" at the runner anyway?

Benches emptied and words were exchanged, but Clemens stayed in the game. The bat incident, however, was what was remembered from the game, not Clemens's eight innings of two-hit, nine-strikeout ball or the Yankees' victory.

Clemens claimed, over and over, that there was no intent. No intelligence, either. Clemens may be The Rocket, but he's no rocket scientist.

1991
MAKE IT A TRIM

On August 15, 1991, Don Mattingly was benched and fined $250 for refusing to cut his hair—which was perilously close to his collar. What a disgrace that Mattingly, one of the best Yankee players during the down years of the 1980s and early '90s, dared let his hair almost touch his collar!

Never mind that Mattingly was the league MVP in 1984, or that he set club records for hits (238) and doubles (53) in a season. Or that he won 10 Golden Glove awards, was the team captain, and was a clubhouse leader who played tough every day.

Apparently manager Stump Merrill forgot all that when he told Mattingly that he would be fined $100 for each day his hair remained "over the line." Three other Yankees, catcher Matt Nokes and pitchers Pascual Perez and Steve Farr, were also warned their hair length violated club policy.

All four got their hair cut, but the story didn't end there. After Mattingly got his hair cut by coach Carl "Hawk" Taylor, a New York radio station auctioned off the locks for charity. A New York cop submitted the winning bid of $3,000.

For his part, Merrill was fired after the season ended for leading the Yankees to a stellar 71–91 record.

1950s
YANKEE SEGREGATION ENDURES

Jackie Robinson broke the color barrier in baseball in 1947, but the Yankees wouldn't have a black player on their squad until eight years later, and would regularly field only one black player until the mid-1960s. The club, dominated by racist management, didn't think their white upper-class fans would pay good money to cheer for black players.

In fact, one-time Yankee co-owner Larry MacPhail had led the uprising against integration when Robinson was poised to enter the league. MacPhail said that bringing black fans to the ball park would "result in lessening the value of several Major League franchises."

In the 1950s, general manager George Weiss was slow to integrate the team, even after pickets were held outside of Yankee headquarters. He signed a handful of black players to minor league contracts, but refused to promote them to the parent club, claiming he'd do so when one of the players met the high Yankee standards. According to Dean Chadwin in *Those Damn Yankees*, Weiss said, "I will never allow a black man to wear a Yankee uniform. Boxholders from Westchester don't want that sort of crowd. They would be offended to sit with [blacks]."

By 1955, however, the pressure was intense for the Yankees to integrate the team, especially with sensational black players such as Robinson playing in Brooklyn and Willie Mays playing for the New York Giants. Elston Howard, who had batted .330 with 22 homers with Toronto in the International League the year before, was the perfect player to break the barrier for the Yankees: He was a talented player, quiet and noncontroversial.

However, for several years, Howard couldn't stay in the same hotel as his teammates during spring training in Florida. And although his teammates supported him, Yankee manager Casey Stengel called him "Eight ball" to his face, in reference to the black pool ball.

1939
DELIBERATE OUTS

On September 3, 1939, the Yankees and Red Sox were in the nightcap of a doubleheader when a 6:30 P.M. Sunday curfew approached.

The Yankees had scored twice in the top of the eighth to take a 7–5 lead, but with the curfew nearing they began making deliberate outs to get to the bottom of the inning. The rules said that if the full inning weren't played before the curfew, the game would revert to the previous inning and end in a 5–5 tie.

There was nothing subtle about what the Yankees were doing. Babe Dahlgren struck out swinging while being given an intentional walk. George Selkirk and Joe Gordon tried to steal home on successive pitches by trotting to home plate.

The normally staid Boston fans, catching on to what the Yankees were doing, showed their displeasure by littering the field with straw hats, soda bottles, seat cushions, and other debris. The umpire ruled that the crowd made it impossible to continue the game and forfeited the contest to New York.

However, American League president Will Harridge saw the farce in the Yankee tactics. He overturned the umpires' decision. And to this day, the game stands as a 5–5 draw.

1983
FOWL BALL

Dave Winfield was charged with cruelty to animals after he hit and killed a low-flying gull in Toronto's Exhibition Stadium while playing catch with a ball boy between innings. When the bird fell to its death, Winfield doffed his cap in mock sorrow for laughs.

But the constable didn't find the matter funny and arrested Winfield in the locker room. The charge was dropped the following day when Canadian prosecutors said there was no criminal intent. Still, Winfield drew the ire of Canadian fans and animal groups.

"All I can tell you is that it's quite unfortunate that a fowl of Canada is no longer with us," Winfield said.

1909
STEALING SIGNS

Stealing signs from opposing coaches and players is as old as baseball. But the Yankees took the thievery to new lows in 1909. That's when, it's been written, Yankee manager George Stallings rented an apartment overlooking right field of the Yankees' home field, Hilltop Park, and placed an agent of the team there.

Using binoculars, the man stole signs from opposing teams and then used mirrors to send the information to Yankee coaches. When Stallings's apartment was found out in 1910, he put a man inside the "O" of a whiskey billboard on the outfield fence. The spy would hold out his hand as a signal—right hand for fastball and left hand for curve.

1981
WORLD SERIES FUTILITY

George Frazier set a World Series record for futility when he lost three games, and compiled an ERA of 17.18, in the 1981 series loss to the Los Angeles Dodgers. He is the only pitcher to ever lose three games in a single World Series.

The humiliation, however, wasn't fully experienced until the following season toward the end of an August doubleheader with the White Sox. With Frazier on the mound at the end of the double-bill, owner George Steinbrenner had the public address announcer offer the 34,000 fans a free ticket to any future home game for having endured a 1–0 loss followed by a 14–2 rout.

Frazier, the losing pitcher in the second game, sat on the mound with his head hung in humiliation.

1921
RUTHIAN RUCKUS

Babe Ruth was a boisterous, carefree soul who didn't like to be told what to do. Mountain Landis was a no-nonsense commissioner who laid down the law and was determined to establish authority over all of baseball.

That was the setting when Ruth and three other Yankees—Bob Meusel, Carl Mays and Wally Schang—planned a barnstorming tour following the 1921 season. Ruth had earned hefty fees for appearing in postseason exhibition tours the previous two years, and wanted to do it again.

But Landis cited a rule that specifically barred members of World Series teams from playing in postseason games. The rule was designed so that exhibition games wouldn't take interest away from the World Series itself in case the two World Series teams decided to travel around the country after the series and play each other. Whether the rule was designed to be applied to individual players didn't matter—a rule was a rule, and Landis was going to enforce it. He ordered Ruth and the others to cancel their plans.

Mays and Schang relented, but Ruth—with his tagalong buddy Meusel in tow—had dollar signs in his eyes and insisted on going.

In the end, Landis got the last laugh. Not only was the exhibition tour a financial flop, but Landis also fined Ruth and Meusel the amount of their World Series shares and suspended them for the first six weeks of the 1922 season. Ruth, in typical fashion, howled in protest, but the suspension stood.

As a result, Ruth didn't play until May 20 the following season, and then played in only 110 games out of the 154-game schedule, causing his statistics to plummet.

1922
RUTHIAN RUCKUS II

On May 25, 1922, Babe Ruth lost his temper, his team captaincy and $200.

On that day, while playing Washington at Yankee Stadium, he was thrown out at second while trying to stretch a single into a double. Ruth responded by throwing dirt into the eyes of umpire George Hildebrand, who then gave the Babe the boot. As he returned to the dugout, fans began booing Ruth; in response, he gave them a theatrical bow.

When one fan's heckling became too much, Ruth jumped onto the dugout roof and into the stands in hot pursuit—but the heckler was faster and made his getaway.

In the book *Babe*, Ruth is said to have looked up into the crowd and shouted, "Come on down and fight! Anyone who wants to fight, come down on the field! Ah, you're all alike—you're all yellow!"

IN THE BOOK "BABE," RUTH IS SAID TO HAVE LOOKED UP INTO THE CROWD AND SHOUTED, "COME ON DOWN AND FIGHT! ANYONE WHO WANTS TO FIGHT, COME DOWN ON THE FIELD! AH, YOU'RE ALL ALIKE— YOU'RE ALL YELLOW!"

For his actions, Ruth was suspended for one game, fined and stripped of his title of team captain. The next month, Ruth drew a two-game suspension for protesting an umpire's calls too vociferously two days in a row.

2003
YANKEE THUGS

Tensions were high between the top and bottom of the ninth inning in game 3 of the American League Championship Series in Boston. Things were so on edge, in fact, that a part-time Fenway Park groundskeeper got mugged—in the Yankee bullpen by two Yankee players, incredibly.

Paul Williams was in the bullpen cheering for the Red Sox when he was approached by relief pitcher Jeff Nelson, who punched Williams in the chest. A police report said Nelson began punching and kicking at Williams, at which point a number of other Yankees jumped on the victim. Right fielder Karim Garcia jumped over the wall into the bullpen to get into the fray. Williams sustained numerous injuries, including what appeared to be cleat marks on his body.

Garcia and Nelson later agreed to a plea deal to perform community service and be evaluated on whether they needed anger management courses. Williams sued the players for medical bills, lost wages and loss of his sense of smell, saying the fight left him with a deviated septum, a neck injury and broken teeth.

1977
THE REGGIE BAR

Before becoming a Yankee, Reggie Jackson once said he would have a candy bar named after him if he played in the Big Apple. He was right. When he joined the club, Standard Brands Confectionary manufactured the Reggie Bar—a bar of chocolate-covered peanuts and caramel in a square orange wrapper with a picture of Reggie swinging a bat.

"THE REGGIE IS THE ONLY CANDY BAR THAT UNWRAPS ITSELF AND TELLS YOU HOW GOOD IT IS," SAID CATFISH HUNTER.

When the bar was introduced, it prompted plenty of remarks about Jackson's egotism. "The Reggie is the only candy bar that unwraps itself and tells you how good it is," said Catfish Hunter. "It's the only candy bar that tastes like a hot dog," quipped another.

On Opening Day of 1978, the Yankees handed out free Reggie Bars to fans. When Jackson boomed a three-run homer in the first inning, the fans exploded with chants of "Reg-gie!" Looking for a way to show their appreciation, they began throwing their candy bars onto the field. For more than five minutes, fans sailed thousands of the bars onto the grass, forcing the umpires to send the grounds crew to clean them up.

After the game, White Sox manager Bob Lemon said someone could have been hurt. Besides, he added, people are hungry elsewhere in the world. "People starving all over the world, and 30 billion calories are laying on the field," he said.

The Reggie Bar was never a hit outside of New York and was discontinued in 1980, the year before Jackson left New York for California. But it inspired limited-edition candy bars for other baseball stars, including Jose Canseco, Ken Griffey Jr., and Wade Boggs, in their hometowns.

1970

BALL FOUR

Jim Bouton was a two-season wonder with the Yankees when he went a combined 39–20 in 1963 and 1964. He was an All-Star and won two World Series games in 1964.

But after four more seasons with the Yankees during which he won a total of only nine games, he was shipped off to the Seattle Pilots. That's where he began keeping a diary of the 1969 season that also exposed the Yankees for what they were in the early and mid-'60s.

Bouton's book, *Ball Four*, was the first tell-all sports book when it hit bookstores in 1970. Although tame by today's standards, the book chronicled how baseball players—*gasp*—liked to drink and smoke and chase women. It told of amphetamines and racial quotas and management hypocrisy in contract negotiations.

The book stunned the sports world and threw players, team executives, sportswriters, and commissioner Bowie Kuhn into a tizzy. Bouton was ostracized, called a Judas. Kuhn tried to force Bouton to sign a statement saying the book was a bunch of lies. One team burned a copy in protest. Pete Rose, a noted baseball gambler who would later be banned for life from Major League Baseball for actions against the game, wasn't alone when he repeatedly shouted, "Fuck you, Shakespeare," at Bouton from the opposing dugout.

For their part, the Yankees and certain Yankee players—Mickey Mantle and Elston Howard among them—vilified Bouton for besmirching their good name. Bouton was blackballed by the Yankees, and it wasn't until 1998, 28 years after the book was published and after a heartfelt letter appeared in *The New York Times* from Bouton's son, that the Yankees "allowed" Bouton to play in an Old-Timers Day game at Yankee Stadium.

1960s
MUDBALLS AND SCUFFBALLS

Whitey Ford won 236 games in his 16-year Yankee career. He just wasn't always fair about it.

Toward the end of his career, "Slick," as he was called, became adept at scuffing balls and applying foreign substances to them. To him, his job was to get batters out any way he could—even if it meant applying some mud to the ball.

One of his favorite tricks involved hiding a tiny rasp on his wedding ring to nick the ball. Ford once explained that the sharp edge cut the ball in such a way that it sank slightly, making it different than his spitter and mudball.

Alvin Dark, manager of Kansas City, put an end to the scuffballs when he collected a bushel of the pitched balls and showed them to umpire Hank Soar, pointing out how they all had the same scuff marks on them. Soar, in turn, ordered Ford to get rid of the ring.

1934
FOUL BALL BRAWL

The Yankees were so cheap that they used to chase down foul balls hit into the stands so they could be used again in the game. The petty practice came to an end at Yankee Stadium after a confrontation between a teenage fan and some ushers.

David Levy was attempting to dig a foul ball hit by Lou Gehrig out of a screen where it had lodged itself. Exuberant Yankee Stadium ushers attacked the boy, fracturing his skull in the process.

Three years later, a federal court awarded Levy $7,500 for his pain. After the court decision, the front office made the decision that any fan could keep foul balls hit into the stands.

> DAVID LEVY WAS ATTEMPTING TO DIG A FOUL BALL HIT BY LOU GEHRIG OUT OF A SCREEN WHERE IT HAD LODGED ITSELF. EXUBERANT YANKEE STADIUM USHERS ATTACKED THE BOY, FRACTURING HIS SKULL IN THE PROCESS.

1977
NO GIRLS ALLOWED

Are the Yankees sexist? It certainly looked that way during the 1977 World Series.

Melissa Ludtke was a reporter for *Sports Illustrated* when she was assigned to cover the 1977 World Series between the Yankees and the Los Angeles Dodgers. She soon became a plaintiff in a lawsuit when she was forbidden from entering the Yankees' locker room to interview players following games.

The Dodgers voted to give Ludtke access to their clubhouse during the World Series, but the Yankees and commissioner Bowie Kuhn wouldn't think of allowing her into the Yanks' locker rooms. Ludtke recalled being told that the clubhouse was off-limits because the players' wives hadn't been consulted, and that if she entered the locker room the players' children would be embarrassed in school the next day.

Sports Illustrated's parent corporation, Time Inc., filed a federal sex discrimination suit against the commissioner, American League president Lee MacPhail, the Yankees, the New York mayor and other New York city officials as owners of Yankee Stadium. U.S. District Judge Constance Baker Motley ruled that women reporters could not be barred from the locker rooms of all New York City sports teams.

The case set precedent for women sports journalists getting the same access as their male colleagues.

"I RECOGNIZE THAT THEY [THE YANKEES] ARE WHAT'S EVIL IN SPORTS. IT'S NOT THAT THERE'S HATRED, BUT THIS IS THE EPICENTER OF ALL THINGS THAT ARE WRONG WITH PROFESSIONAL SPORTS EMBODIED BY GEORGE STEINBRENNER."

—BEN AFFLECK,
ACTOR AND RED SOX FAN

THOSE DAMNED YANKEES

FUN YANKEE FACTS

TEAM RECORDS

- Most runs allowed, season: 898, in 1908.
- Most runs allowed, inning: 13 on June 17, 1925, in a 19–1 loss to Detroit.
- Most hits allowed, game: 28, against Detroit, September 29, 1928.
- Most runs allowed in season by a player: Russ Ford, 165 runs in 1912.
- Most hits allowed in a game by one pitcher: 21, Jack Quinn, to Boston on June 29, 1912.
- Most home runs allowed in a game by one pitcher: 5, Joe Ostrowski, 1950; John Cumberland, 1970; Ron Guidry, 1985; Jeff Weaver, 2002; and David Wells, 2003.
- Most home runs allowed, inning, by one pitcher: 4, Catfish Hunter against Boston on June 17, 1977, and Scott Sanderson against Minnesota on May 2, 1992.
- Most home runs allowed by a pitcher, season: 40, Ralph Terry in 1962.
- Most home runs allowed by a pitcher, career: 228, Whitey Ford.
- Most losses by a pitcher, season: 22, Joe Lake in 1908.
- Most strikeouts, season: 1,171 in 2002 (an average of more than 7 Ks per game).
- Most strikeouts, season, by a player: 157, Alfonso Soriano in 2002.

- Most strikeouts, season, by a left-handed batting player: 133, Reggie Jackson in 1978.
- Most strikeouts, season, by a switch hitter: 151, Jorge Posada in 2000.
- Most strikeouts, career: 1,710, Mickey Mantle. (That far outdistances the second-best strikeout king in club history, Babe Ruth, who whiffed 1,122 times.)
- Most strikeouts, game, team: 17, September 10, 1999, against Boston's Pedro Martinez.
- Lowest slugging percentage, team: .287, in 1914.
- Fewest home runs, season, team: 8, in 1913.
- Most losses in a season: 103, in 1908.
- Most losses at home: 47, in 1908.
- Fewest wins at home: 27, in 1913.
- Fewest wins on the road: 19, in 1912.
- Most times shut out, season: 27, in 1914.
- Highest ERA, season: 4.88, in 1930.
- Most runs allowed, game: 24, July 29, 1928, vs. Cleveland.
- Most runs allowed, inning: 13, June 17, 1925, vs. Detroit.
- Most hits allowed, game: 28, September 29, 1928, vs. Detroit.
- Most homers allowed, game: 7, July 4, 2003, vs. Boston.
- Most walks allowed, game: 19, September 11, 1949, vs. Washington.
- Most walks allowed, season: 812, in 1949.
- Most runners left on base, game: 20, September 21, 1956, vs. Boston.
- Most errors, season: 386, in 1912.
- Fewest stolen bases, season: 24, in 1948.
- Most times caught stealing, season: 82, in 1920.

SIXTH INNING

AP Photo

Previous page—Kansas City Royals fans voice their opinion, shared by many, about Yankees owner George Steinbrenner at Kauffman Stadium in Kansas City on April 30, 1999. The mega-rich Yankee payroll dwarfs what the small-market Royals can afford to pay.

OWNERS

From a gambling kingpin to a convicted felon with an addiction to meddling, the Yankees have enjoyed a long history of colorful team owners.

The Yankees franchise was originally brought to New York by an ownership team composed of a gambler and a grafter. The team then passed to a pair that rarely saw eye to eye and whose bickersome ways led to their split. The next team of owners was a trio, one of whom went crazy at a team party and sold his shares the next day.

In the mid-1960s, a media conglomerate purchased the team, setting off fears it would interfere with Major League Baseball's TV contract or draw the ire of federal regulators. And finally, an investment team headed by shipping magnate George Steinbrenner bought the Yankees in 1973. The first words out of Steinbrenner's mouth were a lie.

THE GAMBLER AND THE CORRUPT COP (1903–1914)

In 1903, Frank Farrell and William "Big Bill" Devery purchased the defunct Baltimore franchise of the American League for $18,000 and moved the team to Manhattan. And thus, the first ownership team of the Yankees included a gambler and corrupt cop.

Devery was a former New York City police chief whose political connections were enough for American League president Ban Johnson to ignore his reputation for corruption and accept him as co-owner of the Highlanders.

He was the silent partner to Frank Farrell, a gambling kingpin who was said to have run a network of 200 gambling outlets and kept a host of local politicians on his payroll.

Devery at first preferred to run his real-estate empire with the payoff money he had accepted as police chief, but after 1908 he became more active in the club and sided with Hal Chase—a known gambler who threw baseball games—in a feud with the team's manager.

By the time Farrell and Devery unloaded the team, the franchise was in disarray, attendance was dismal, and Devery and Farrell were losing money and blaming each other for it.

THE ODD COUPLE (1915-1945)

In 1915, Colonel Jacob Ruppert and Colonel Tillinghast L'Hommedieu "Cap" Huston purchased the team—even though both men were admittedly fans of the New York Giants. In fact, the two colonels wanted to buy the Giants and only turned to the Yankees when the Giants weren't available.

The pair made for an odd couple. Ruppert was a wealthy New York brewer and sportsman, a polished socialite and an honorary colonel on the staff of the New York governor. He was said to have bought the team as a promotional stunt and intended to name it the Knickerbockers after his brewery's best-selling beer. But sports editors at New York papers refused to go along because the name was too long to fit in headlines.

Huston was a rumpled Army Corps of Engineers captain who made his money in Cuba following the Spanish-American War.

The pair disagreed from the beginning, including on how Huston put up his half of the purchase price in $100 bills. How gauche!

92

The biggest disagreement between the two came in 1918. Huston became incensed when Ruppert didn't consult him when he hired Miller Huggins as manager before the 1918 season. Huston wanted to hire his friend, former Brooklyn Dodger coach Wilbert Robinson, but—as was usually the case in his eight and a half years as co-owner of the team—he didn't get his way.

Huston managed to ruffle a few feathers of his own. During World War I, he wrote letters to newspapers suggesting that Major League Baseball be shut down and all the players shipped to the front lines.

In 1922, Ruppert bought out Huston for $1.5 million. It was an unprecedented sum at the time, but Ruppert felt he needed complete control for the team to win.

Ruppert retained control of the team until his death in 1939, and the team remained in the family estate until 1945.

THE THREE STOOGES (1945–1965)

In 1945, Del Webb, Dan Topping and Larry MacPhail purchased the team for $2.8 million from the estate of the late Col. Jacob Ruppert. Webb and Topping bought out MacPhail's share just two years later.

MacPhail—who had formerly been general manager of the Reds and chief operating officer of the Dodgers—is credited with turning the franchise into a bloodless corporate machine.

His manner led Joe McCarthy and Bill Dickey to resign as managers. He bought a plane for the team to travel in, but it was a rickety military transport plane with questionable flying ability that many players refused to fly in.

MacPhail also opposed integration. He claimed blacks didn't have the discipline to play in the Major Leagues, that integration would hurt the Negro Leagues, and that white fans wouldn't pay to watch games with blacks. He had been making a few extra bucks arranging off-season all-star games between Major Leaguers and stars from the Negro Leagues, and he thought radio and TV ad money would dry up if there was a racially mixed audience.

After the World Series in 1947, MacPhail apparently had a mental breakdown of sorts when in a drunken stupor he unleashed a barrage of insults and punches at a victory party. The next day, he sold his share of the team.

Topping and Webb, both of them multimillionaires, then sowed the seeds that would lead to the Yankees' eventual decline in the 1960s. They made a series of ill-advised moves with their managers and forced out manager Casey Stengel—who had won 10 pennants and seven World Series—after the 1960 World Series. General manager George Weiss, seeing the writing on the wall, resigned a couple of months later.

When Topping and Webb decided they wanted to sell the team, they stopped spending money on their farm system—setting up the franchise for a fall the likes of which had rarely been seen before. When CBS offered to buy 80 percent of the team in 1964 for $11.2 million, the other team owners in Major League Baseball approved the deal only after Topping and Webb assured them they would continue to run the team for five years.

But the ink was barely dry on the sales contract when Webb sold his remaining 10 percent in February 1965. Topping held out for another 18 months before selling his remaining shares.

Webb attempted to get back into baseball in the early 1970s when he made a pitch for the Chicago White Sox. But the deal fell apart because he refused to divest his holdings in several Las Vegas casinos, a condition of the sale imposed by baseball commissioner Bowie Kuhn.

THE EYE BLINKS (1965–1973)

CBS certainly picked the wrong time to make an investment in the New York Yankees.

As soon as CBS bought the New York Yankees, the team collapsed. Fresh off a World Series appearance the season before, the Yankees finished 25 games out of first place in 1965. The next year, the team fell into the American League cellar with a .440 winning percentage—the sorriest record since 1913.

During CBS's tenure as owner, the team was known for little else other than bad and mediocre teams. Even in its best year during CBS's ownership, the club finished 15 games out of first place.

In 1972, attendance fell to under one million, the lowest total since 1945 when the nation was winding down from World War II.

CBS eventually decided that it should stick to TV and radio, and put the team up for sale. When the $10-million sale was completed, to an investment team led by an unknown personality named George Steinbrenner, CBS was out of baseball—at a loss of $4 million.

THE BOSS: KING GEORGE (1973–PRESENT)

When shipping magnate George Steinbrenner assembled a team of investors and bought the Yankees in 1973, he vowed he wouldn't be active in the day-to-day operations of the team. So much for promises.

In the three-plus decades that he has owned the Yankees, Steinbrenner has proven to be an intrusive owner of unmatched proportions. Not since Connie Mack—who not only owned the Philadelphia Athletics but managed them as well—has a team owner put his fingers so mercilessly into the daily machinations of his team.

Unpredictable and spontaneous, Steinbrenner has hired and fired managers nearly two dozen times, making for a revolving door to the manager's office. He has been suspended from baseball for consorting with a two-bit gambler. He was convicted for making illegal campaign contributions to Richard Nixon. He became infamous in his pursuit of high-priced free agents in his quest to win at any cost.

And in the process, this fact is often overlooked: George Steinbrenner has lost more games as Yankee owner than any of the five previous ownerships. Through 2004, his teams had lost more than 2,200 games. His teams suffered through the longest drought—13 years—between championships of any Yankees team since their first World Series appearance in 1921.

Steinbrenner made his fortune in shipbuilding, but has long had a passion for sports. In 1960 he bought the Cleveland Pipers of the National Industrial Basketball League. The team later joined the American Basketball League, but Steinbrenner was unable to raise enough money to join the NBA and the team eventually went bankrupt.

In 1972, Steinbrenner offered to buy the Cleveland Indians for $9 million, but was turned down. That set the stage for the following year, when he assembled an investment team to buy the Yankees from CBS. At the time, he said: "I won't be active in the day-to-day-operations of the club, at all."

When free agency became an undeniable part of the game, Steinbrenner said he was dead set against it. "It can ruin the game," he said. He then proceeded to go out and sign Catfish Hunter to a four-year contract for $2.85 million—an unheard-of sum back then.

He picked up Reggie Jackson, too, and the Yankees went on to win three straight pennants—and the World Series in 1977 and 1978—reinforcing for Steinbrenner that the Yankee way of buying championships was the right way. Over the next half century, he loaded up on scores of free agents—many of them overrated or over the hill.

Steinbrenner has embarrassed the team and the league from the start. Barely a year after taking the reins of the franchise, he was indicted on 14 counts for illegal campaign contributions to Richard Nixon and others. Four months later he pleaded guilty to two counts, making illegal contributions and obstruction, and was fined $20,000. He was a convicted felon. Commissioner Bowie Kuhn suspended him from the league for two years, but the suspension later was reduced.

Steinbrenner was cleansed of his felony sins when he was pardoned by President Ronald Reagan in January 1989. Steinbrenner had tried to clear his record before, but then-president Jimmy Carter rejected his plea for a pardon.

Commissioner Fay Vincent then banned Steinbrenner from running the Yankees for life after it was discovered that Steinbrenner had paid a gambler, Howard Spira, $40,000 to find dirt on Dave Winfield. When that ban was announced, fans responded with a standing ovation at Yankee Stadium. Spira was later sentenced to two and a half years in prison for trying to extort $110,000 from the Yankees organization. Three years later, however, Steinbrenner was reinstated to baseball after team owners fired Vincent as commissioner.

Dubbed "The Boss" by the New York media, Steinbrenner has been in constant turmoil with—well, everybody. He was fined $50,000 for criticizing umpires during a playoff series with Seattle. He once got into a fight with two fans in a hotel elevator, emerging with a broken hand and a fat lip. He has publicly embarrassed his own players and taken potshots at rivals.

THIRD BASEMAN GRAIG NETTLES ONCE SUMMED UP PLAYERS' SENTIMENTS TOWARD STEINBRENNER WHEN HE SAID, "THE MORE WE LOSE, THE MORE HE'LL FLY IN. AND THE MORE HE FLIES IN, THE BETTER CHANCE THAT THERE'LL BE A PLANE CRASH."

Third baseman Graig Nettles once summed up players' sentiments toward Steinbrenner when he said, "The more we lose, the more he'll fly in. And the more he flies in, the better chance that there'll be a plane crash."

Steinbrenner has proven over and over that he can't be held to his word. In 1985, he gave skipper Yogi Berra a vote of confidence, saying that Berra would remain the manager for the rest of the season regardless of how badly the club played. Sixteen games later, Berra was fired.

After the Yankees acquired Alex Rodriguez following the Red Soxs' failure to do so, Steinbrenner took a verbal blast at Sox owner John Henry. "Unlike the Yankees, he chose not to go the extra distance for his fans in Boston. It is understandable, but wrong that he would try to deflect the accountability for his mistakes on to others and to a system for which he voted in favor. It is time to get on with life and forget the sour grapes."

A few months later, as all Yankee haters know, the Red Sox defeated the Yankees in the American League Championship Series when the Yanks dropped four straight after leading the series, three games to none. Rodriguez was a flop, and justice was served.

"HATING THE YANKEES ISN'T PART OF MY ACT. IT IS ONE OF THOSE EXQUISITE TIMES WHEN LIFE AND ART ARE IN PERFECT CONJUNCTION."

BILL VEECK,
OWNER, CHICAGO WHITE SOX

NOW BATTING . . .

TOM CARON

Yankees suck!

That's the rallying cry for an entire region of people. Good people who make peace, not war, scream it out at the top of their lungs. Peaceful souls who teach their children to love each other wear "Yankee Hater" hats. It is one of the unifying beliefs for a far-flung group of people dubbed "Red Sox Nation" by *Boston Globe* columnist Dan Shaughnessy.

Why do we hate them so much?

Is it simply because they win? Is it because they won 26 World Championships between 1923 and 2000, while the Red Sox won exactly zero during that same stretch? Is it because they are one of the true dynasties in all of sports?

Yes. It is for all of those reasons—but also for so many more.

It is because of everything they have been, and everything our team has not been, for so many years. They were the hammer, we

YANKEES SUCK!
THAT'S THE RALLYING CRY FOR AN ENTIRE REGION OF PEOPLE. GOOD PEOPLE WHO MAKE PEACE, NOT WAR, SCREAM IT OUT AT THE TOP OF THEIR LUNGS. PEACEFUL SOULS WHO TEACH THEIR CHILDREN TO LOVE EACH OTHER WEAR "YANKEE HATER" HATS.

were the nail. They were the boot, we were the sidewalk. They were the boxer, we were the punching bag.

They won. We lost. Again and again and again. How can you not hate that?

There's no question that we, as Red Sox fans, are born into the emotions that color our summers. When the Sox win, the summer nights are long, warm, and happy. When the Sox win and the Yankees lose, those nights are even better. When the Sox beat the Yankees, those summer nights are positively euphoric. Winter is years away.

Of course, there have been many games when it went the other way: Saturday afternoons where the New Yorkers crushed the Bostonians and spoiled another perfectly good summer weekend.

There are 19 cataclysmic battles between the Sox and Yankees every summer. Twenty-six head-to-head battles, if you include the inevitable postseason meeting in the American League Championship Season.

Familiarity breeds contempt. And we are already very familiar with these Yankees. After all, we saw one of the greatest home-run hitters in baseball history leave Boston for New York decades ago. We watched New York raise banner after banner. We watched former Sox stalwarts like Roger Clemens and Wade Boggs go to Yankee Stadium to win their elusive first World Championships.

It's one thing to lose to a rival; it's another thing to have it rubbed in your face year after year after year. It's only natural to hate that.

So we hate. We hate pinstripes. We hate the House that Ruth Built. We hate the owner, the front office, the players. We hate Ronan Tynan, the wonderful Irish tenor who sings "God Bless America" during the seventh-inning stretch at the Stadium.

However, all that was before we were freed from 86 years of domination. The Red Sox won it all in 2004, and did it by charging back from a 3–0 series deficit against the Yankees. The Sox were the first team in Major League Baseball history to mount such a comeback.

They stun the Yankees, win the Series, and then raise the banner in front of New York at the 2005 Fenway opener. It is Bizarro Baseball World, where everything is upside down.

So, we should be over our hate now. The Yankees are still our ultimate rival, but they're chasing us. Let them fester in hatred. No such luck.

In response to 2004, New York went out and got Randy Johnson. I think I'm going to hate him in pinstripes . . .

Tom Caron is the studio host of Boston Red Sox baseball telecasts on the New England Sports Network (NESN), anchoring the network's pre- and postgame coverage. He is a Lewiston, Maine, native and grew up hating the Yankees.

SEVENTH INNING

Previous page—Ted Williams, the greatest hitter who ever lived and an American icon who has been called the real-life John Wayne, in 1941. Williams finished his career with tremendous statistics despite missing nearly five seasons during his prime to serve in World War II and the Korean War. In the 1940s, he lost out on three possible MVP awards, due at least in part to Yankee bias and favoritism as well as his stormy relationship with the baseball media.

ALL THE (YANKEE) BREAKS

From Babe Ruth to Alex Rodriguez, the gilded bully-boy Yankees have long excelled at getting things their way.

Call it deception, favoritism, partiality, trickery, or dishonesty—or maybe it's downright scamming, conning or fraud. However you look at it, the franchise has benefited mightily from bad umpire calls, dirty tricks, undeserved awards and, of course, the most famous sports curse in history.

1920
BABE RUTH SOLD TO YANKEES

This is the spring from which all Yankee success flows. Boston Red Sox owner Harry Frazee preferred Broadway over baseball, which helps explain how the New York Yankees, an absolutely miserable franchise for nearly two decades, bought the greatest player ever and officially ushered in the Yankee tradition of buying success.

Frazee, a theatrical producer in need of money to finance a Broadway show, sold Ruth after the 1919 season to the Yankees for $125,000 in cash, plus a loan of $350,000. It apparently wasn't enough for Frazee that Ruth had helped lead the Sox to World Series victories in 1915, 1916, and 1918. It didn't matter to him that it was already clear that Ruth would change the face of baseball.

As a pitcher in 1916, Ruth won 23 games for the Sox and led the league in ERA (1.75) and shutouts (9). In the 1918 World Series, he pitched 16 consecutive scoreless innings, running his streak to 29 scoreless innings in a row, a World Series record that stood for 43 years.

But as great a pitcher as he was, he was an even better batter. So, in 1919, he began to play every day, not only pitching but also playing the outfield. He pitched in 17 games, going 9–5 with a 2.97 ERA, but was even more impressive at the plate. He shattered the single-season home-run record by hitting 29, 19 more than the second-place finisher that year. He drove in a league-leading 114 runs and had a .456 on-base percentage and a .657 slugging percentage. He single-handedly changed the game and ushered in the home-run era.

Yet, that December he was gone—and baseball history was dramatically changed. In 1920, his first season with the Yankees, he bested his own home-run mark by hitting an amazing 54 home runs, 35 more than the second-place finisher and more than all but one *team* managed to hit that year.

With the Yankees, of course, Ruth went on to become the most dominant force baseball has ever seen and the best player in Major League history. He rewrote the record books. He was larger than life and was idolized by fans, who flocked to ballparks to see him play. It was his drawing power that generated enormous gate receipts and cash for the Yankees. In his first year with the Yankees, the team became the first franchise to draw more than one million fans. And it was that drawing power that prompted Yankee owners to build Yankee Stadium—still known as The House that Ruth Built. With its 62,000 seating capacity, it was the largest in the country. Which meant even *more* money, and the official coming-out party of the Evil Empire.

For his part, Frazee, who was in constant need of money, systematically dismantled the league's first dynasty and sold the team's best players—often to the Yankees. He bought the Red Sox for $400,000 when they were World Champions in 1917. By the time he sold them, just six years later in 1923, they were a last-place team and doomed to stay also-rans until the arrival of Ted Williams in 1939. They would not win another World Series title for 86 years.

1942
THE KID GETS SHAFTED

In 1942, Theodore Samuel "The Kid" Williams, the greatest hitter who ever lived, won the Triple Crown with 36 home runs, 137 RBIs and a .356 batting average. Nonetheless, it was Joe "Flash" Gordon, the Yankees' second baseman, who won Most Valuable Player award that year. In true Yankee fashion, the team was the beneficiary of another team or player's unrightful loss.

The undeserving Gordon, who led the league in errors by a second baseman that year, hit .322 with 18 home runs and 103 RBIs. Although it was a career-best batting average for Gordon, the numbers paled in comparison to those of Williams.

For part of that year, Williams was under fire in the press for playing baseball while his country was at war. Williams enlisted in the Naval Aviation Service on May 22, 1942, and would report for duty at the end of the season. Among other reasons, he wanted to play the season to earn enough money to help support his mother, for whom he was essentially the sole source of income. Williams would lose three full seasons in his prime to military service in World War II and then lose another season and a half to serve in Korea. Those nearly five seasons lost cost him any chance to break some of Babe Ruth's career records, including home runs. Williams finished with 521.

Just compare these numbers.

1942	BA	H	HR	RBI	Slugging	On-base Avg.
Williams	.356	186	36	137	.648	.499
Gordon	.322	173	18	103	.491	.409

It was the writers who voted on the MVP. So even though Williams won the Triple Crown, he finished second to a Yankee in the MVP voting. In the now-legendary baseball year of 1941, Williams hit .406, making him the last player to break the famed .400 mark. Meanwhile, media darling Joe DiMaggio won the MVP award on the back of his record 56-game hitting streak. Despite DiMaggio's hot streak, it was Ted who led the league with an astonishing .553 on-base percentage (113 points *higher* than DiMaggio), led the league in home runs with 37 and slugging percentage at .735 (nearly 100 points *higher* than DiMaggio).

Here are the statistical facts for 1941:

	BA	H	HR	RBI	Slugging	On-base
Williams	.406	185	37	120	.735	.553
DiMaggio	.357	193	30	125	.643	.440

1947
THE KID GETS SHAFTED—PART II

Ted Williams again was passed over for MVP in 1947, even though he *again* won the Triple Crown, hitting .343 with 32 dingers and 114 RBIs. This time the recipient was *again* Joe DiMaggio, even though his numbers were *again* inferior. DiMaggio finished the year with a .315 batting average, 20 homers and 97 RBIs—which weren't even close to the Kid's Triple Crown numbers. In addition, Williams led the league in on-base percentage, slugging average, runs scored, and total bases. He finished the year ahead of DiMaggio in every significant statistical category, often by a wide margin. Ahhh, New York.

1947	BA	H	HR	RBI	Slugging	On-base
Williams	.343	181	32	114	.634	.499
DiMaggio	.315	168	20	97	.522	.391

Two baseball legends meet in 1943—Ted Williams and Babe Ruth.

1996
HOOKY-PLAYING HERO

Jeffrey Maier was just a 12-year-old kid from Jersey who cut school to see his beloved Yankees take on the Orioles in the opener of the American League Championship Series in 1996. By the end of the day, he was a hero, and the answer to a trivia question in the team's history of getting things their way by any means necessary—and especially at the expense of others.

With the Yankees trailing 4–3 in the bottom of the eighth, Derek Jeter lofted a fly ball to the right-field wall, where Tony Tarasco was poised to make the catch. Instead, Maier reached over the wall with his glove and snatched the ball out of midair. Replays clearly showed Maier extended his arm into the field of play and that by rule Jeter should have been out, but umpire Richie Garcia gave Jeter a homer.

"And they're going to call it a home run, I can't believe it," the radio announcer said. "Richie Garcia is calling it a home run and Tarasco is out to argue. A terrible call by Richie Garcia."

ESPN has ranked Garcia's blunder as the fourth-worst call in sports history. After later reviewing the video, even Garcia admitted he probably should have called fan interference. Instead, the game went into extra innings, with New York winning on Bernie Williams's homer in the 11th.

Meanwhile, Maier became a celebrity among Yankee fans. More than a dozen reporters and cameramen surrounded him in his hometown of Old Tappan, New Jersey, the next day as his parents escorted him to school. The principal decided not to punish him for skipping school. The Old Tappan Deli offered a Jeff Maier Special—a turkey sandwich, cherry Coke and small pretzels—for $4.75. He appeared on *Good Morning America* and *Live With Regis and Kathie Lee*, but turned down *Geraldo*.

In Baltimore, officials jokingly suggested that Maier should be arrested. "That's grand theft and it's bookable in Baltimore," police commissioner Thomas Frazier said. The mayor opened his weekly news conference by saying the play proved that New York didn't have a zero-tolerance policy toward crime. "We were robbed and they saw it and nobody did anything about it," he said.

1960
MOST VALUABLE LOSER

The 1960 World Series ended with Bill Mazeroski's unforgettable ninth-inning homer, which gave the underdog Pittsburgh Pirates an improbable World Championship over the heavily favored Yankees.

Even so, it was Yankee second baseman Bobby Richardson—not Mazeroski or a teammate of his—who won the Most Valuable Player honors for the series.

Richardson won the MVP with a .367 batting average, 12 RBIs and a memorable first inning in game 3 when he had a two-run single followed by a grand slam.

But nobody can argue that Mazeroski's home run on a 1–0 pitch is one of the clutch performances in the history of sports, not just baseball. Only a Yankee could be considered the Most Valuable Player of a series in which the Yankees not only went down to defeat, but lost in such dramatic fashion.

1999
PHANTOM TAG

Red Sox fans had to have been shaking their heads at umpire calls that went the Yankees' way during game 4 of the 1999 American League Championship Series.

That's when Yankee second baseman Chuck Knoblauch made a phantom tag that missed a Boston base runner by at least a foot, but umpire Tim Tschida still called an out. The knucklehead call killed Boston's eighth-inning rally, shifted momentum to the Yankees and allowed New York to go on to win the game and the series.

The Yankees were nursing a 3–2 lead when John Valentin hit a slow roller to Knoblauch, who then clearly missed Jose Offerman with the tag before throwing to first to get Valentin. With the bad call, the play ended up being an inning-ending double-play with Nomar Garciaparra due up. A sign reading "Tschida Tsucks" was later seen at Fenway Park.

Tschida later admitted his blunder, but it was too late. The call was all the more exasperating following a horrendous call in the series opener that also went the Yankees' way.

In that game, second-base umpire Rick Reed failed to call an out when Knoblauch dropped a throw. The correct call would have given the Red Sox two on and no outs in the 10th inning with the score tied. Bernie Williams ended up winning the game with a home run in the bottom of the inning.

1976
THE YANKEE WAY: SUCKER PUNCHES

In the bottom of the sixth inning at Yankee Stadium on May 20, 1976, a close play at home plate precipitated what is regarded as the worst on-field fight in the long feud between New York and Boston.

It started when Yankee Lou Piniella barreled cleats-first into Red Sox catcher Carlton Fisk. Both players came up swinging, and the benches cleared for a melee. In the end, it was Sox pitcher Bill Lee, a well-known Yankee killer on the mound, who got the short end of the stick.

Lee, who was backing up home plate when the fight began, was thrown down and had his shoulder ground into the turf by Yankee third baseman Graig Nettles.

Films showed that Mickey Rivers then pounded away at Lee under a pile of bodies, and that when Lee was finally able to get up and throw a punch, his arm was shot. He had suffered a torn ligament in his shoulder, and when he tried to deliver a blow to Nettles, he couldn't raise his arm above his belt. Nettles retaliated with a flurry of punches and was helped by Rivers, who sucker punched Lee in the back.

Lee later said that he didn't think the Yankees started the fight to get him, but once it began they came looking for him. It probably didn't help that Lee at one time said the Yankees had the fighting ability of a "bunch of hookers swinging their purses."

A three-time 17-game winner, Lee was never the same. His fastball disappeared after the injury, and the Red Sox, always in need of pitching, lost their ace lefty. Lee was sent to the bullpen after his return to the team that summer. After two subpar seasons in 1977 and 1978, times when the Red Sox desperately needed a good left-handed arm, Lee was traded to the Montreal Expos, where he finished out his career.

"All literary men are Red Sox fans—To be a Yankee fan in a literate society is to endanger your life."

John Cheever, Author

Fun Yankee Facts

- Reggie Jackson holds the Major League record for most career strikeouts: 2,597.
- Billy Johnson holds the record for hitting into the most double plays in a season by a rookie. He did it 27 times in 1943.
- Johnny Broaca struck out five times in a single game on June 25, 1934, tying a Major League record. Bernie Williams matched Broaca's record in 1991.
- Jim "Catfish" Hunter shares the Major League record for most home runs given up in a single inning, when he gave up four dingers in the first inning on May 17, 1977. Scott Sanderson repeated the record on May 2, 1992, when the Twins took him deep four times in the fifth inning at Yankee Stadium.
- Tommy Byrne led the big leagues for a record five straight years (1948–52) in hit batsmen. In 1949, Byrne walked 179 batters in 196 innings, the worst ratio of bases on balls to innings pitched in Major League history.
- Hal Chase holds the American League record for most errors by a first baseman in a career, with 285.
- Joe Gordon is tied with two others for the most seasons leading American League second basemen in errors. Gordon set the standard in 1938, 1941, 1942 and 1943.
- Mickey Mantle holds the career record for most strikeouts in the World Series, with 54.
- Whitey Ford holds the career record for most bases on balls issued during World Series games, with 34.

- George Pipgras holds the record for strikeouts—five—in a single World Series game, which he set in 1932.
- Bill Bevens gave up a record 10 walks in a World Series game on October 3, 1947.
- Andy Pettitte tied a World Series record for giving up the most earned runs, seven, in a World Series game on October 20, 1996.

SEVENTH-INNING STRETCH

Previous page—Babe Ruth in a Boston Red Sox uniform. Ruth, one of the best left-handed pitchers in baseball, played for the Sox from 1914 to 1919, and helped lead them to three World Series titles. During his last season with the Sox, he switched mostly to the outfield and became the game's most dominant hitter. When the Yankees bought him for cash after the 1919 season (and followed up by purchasing other Sox players from the team's cash-strapped owner), the history of baseball was dramatically and irrevocably changed forever.

GREED

It's not by accident that right-thinking people often utter the words "Yankees" and "greed" in the same breath. In the Yankee mind, money makes the world go round. And just when you think that the team's greed has reached its limit, the club ups the ante with yet another outlandish act.

It has been this way since the beginning. Since acquiring Ruth, the Yankees have essentially always had more money and more power than anyone else in baseball. And they have used it to rule baseball by building a farm system and controlling players in the pre-free agency days, preying on small-market teams, and simply spending cash in the free-agency era. This fact is clear enough: Yankee success has been bought and paid for.

2004—THE $183-MILLION PAYROLL

Nobody spends money more lavishly than the New York Yankees. Back in his heyday, Babe Ruth earned unprecedented amounts. In 1922, the team gave Ruth $52,000 a year because, as Ruth liked to say, he always wanted to make a grand a week. His salary rose to $70,000 a year in the late 1920s, and to $80,000 a year in the early 1930s. By comparison, when Ruth retired, the second-highest salary in the league was that of teammate Lou Gehrig, who made $30,000 annually.

But that was peanuts compared to what modern-day Yankees make. The payroll on Opening Day 2004 was a staggering $183 million—or nearly $8 million per player—and that doesn't include so-called luxury tax payments for exceeding the league's competitive balance threshold.

Overall, the Yankees payroll was nearly $60 million more than the second-highest Major League payroll, and was more than twice that of all but four other teams. In fact, salaries for the team's two highest-paid players alone—Alex Rodriguez and Derek Jeter—was higher than the salaries for the entire team rosters of Milwaukee, Tampa Bay and Cleveland.

Unfortunately for the 2004 Yankees, none of the players were named Ruth or Gehrig. And for the money, the group proved to be the greatest bunch of underachievers in history.

The top-paid players and their salaries in 2004 were:

- Alex Rodriguez: $21.7 million
- Derek Jeter: $18.6 million
- Mike Mussina: $16.0 million
- Kevin Brown: $15.7 million
- Jason Giambi: $12.4 million
- Bernie Williams: $12.4 million
- Gary Sheffield: $12.0 million
- Mariano Rivera: $10.9 million
- Jorge Posada: $9 million
- Javier Vazquez: $9 million
- John Olerud: $7.7 million
- Hideki Matsui: $7 million
- Steve Karsay: $6.0 million

For all that money, not a single Yankee in 2004 hit above .300. Not a single pitcher reached 15 wins. And when it counted most, the team folded in the greatest playoff collapse in Major League history when it lost to the Red Sox in the League Championship Series after streaking to a 3–0 lead in games.

For a staggering $21.7 million, A-Rod was but third on the team in RBIs and fifth in batting average. Miguel Cairo, who had

a $900,000 salary—or less than 5 percent of Rodriguez's pay—
had a higher average.

For $18.6 million, Jeter didn't even drive in 80 runs, and suf-
fered through an 0-for-32 slump in April, the worst batting
swoon by a Yankee player since 1977.

For $16.0 million, Mike Mussina won 12 games, for a payoff
of more than $1.3 million per win. His 4.59 ERA was good
enough for 56th best in the majors.

Kevin Brown did even better for his $15.7 million, winning
just 10 games and having an ERA over 4.00. The highlight of
Brown's year was when he had a temper tantrum following a bad
outing in September and broke his hand when he punched out a
wall in the clubhouse. A New York tabloid carried the headline,
"Brown the Clown."

For $12.4 million, Jason Giambi appeared in just 80 games,
hitting .208 with 12 homers and 40 RBIs. That's $1 million per
homer.

For his money, Bernie Williams hit .262—far off his career
average of .305 and the lowest since his rookie season of 1991.

The lack of accomplishments goes on and on, but it was
Steve Karsay who got the best deal of all. Plagued with injuries,
Karsay appeared in just seven games, pitching 6.2 innings for an
astounding payoff of nearly $1 million per inning pitched. Now
there's a bargain.

2005—$200 MILLION AND CLIMBING

Fresh off the greatest postseason collapse in baseball history—
despite having the highest team payroll in baseball history—the
2005 season saw Steinbrenner open his wallet again and shatter
his own previous payroll record. The gluttonous off-season moves
by the Yankees only added continued evidence that the club oper-
ates using a bottomless pit of moola, and is willing to spend any
amount to buy itself a championship regardless of its effect on
Major League baseball.

When the club signed five-time Cy Young Award winner Randy "Big Unit" Johnson to a deal that pays him nearly $50 million through 2010 (including deferred payments), it helped push the 2005 payroll to roughly $208 million.

That's greater than the gross national product of some small African and South Pacific nations. That's the combined average pay of some 4,400 U.S. teachers. That's eight times as much as it cost to build the Empire State Building. That's a lot of money!

Prior to signing the Big Unit, the Yankees also inked pitcher Carl Pavano to a four-year deal worth $40 million, and pitcher Jaret Wright to a three-year $21-million contract.

Steinbrenner's latest spending spree pushed the payroll to more than $70 million above baseball's so-called "competitive balance tax" threshold. For exceeding the limit for a third time, the Yankees have to pay about a 40 percent tax on the amount over the threshold, which amounts to more than $28 million. The tax alone is higher than the 2004 payroll for the entire Tampa Bay Devil Rays roster.

The Yankees were the only team to pay the luxury tax the first year it was implemented, in 2003, when it owed $11.8 million. In 2004, the Yankees had to pay $25 million. In 2005, combining the tax payment and salaries together means the Yankees will have a payroll of nearly one-quarter of a billion dollars.

By comparison, the Yankees' payroll is some $84 million higher than the second-highest-paid team, the Red Sox, and more than seven times higher than the team with the lowest salary, the Tampa Bay Devil Rays.

The inequity between the Yankees and the rest of the league is stunning. According to the *USA Today* salaries database, here are some payrolls from opening day 2005, including their Major League rankings on the pay scale:

1.	New York Yankees	$208.31 million
2.	Boston Red Sox	$123.51 million
3.	New York Mets	$101.31 million
4.	Los Angeles Angels	$ 97.73 million
5.	Philadelphia Phillies	$ 95.52 million
. . .		
14.	Baltimore Orioles	$ 73.18 million
15.	Detroit Tigers	$ 69.10 million
16.	San Diego Padres	$ 63.30 million
. . .		
26.	Cleveland Indians	$ 45.72 million
27.	Milwaukee Brewers	$ 39.93 million
28.	Pittsburgh Pirates	$ 38.13 million
29.	Kansas City Royals	$ 36.89 million
30.	Tampa Bay Devil Rays	$ 29.36 million

Consider this: In 2005, the entire Tampa Bay team will be paid only $3.36 million more than Alex Rodriguez's $26-million salary.

RAIDING THE RED SOX

Babe Ruth wasn't the only player the Yankees bought from the Red Sox. In the early 1920s, the Yankees used cash to stock its lineup with former Boston players as it began winning pennants and World Series.

Even before the team landed Ruth, the Yankees got pitcher Carl Mays—who had won a combined 61 games the three previous seasons—from the Red Sox midway through the 1919 campaign for $40,000, as well as three journeyman pitchers. Mays proceeded to win 26 games in pinstripes in 1920 and 27 games the following season.

Then came the January 1920 Babe Ruth deal (the biggest and most one-sided swap in baseball history), when the Yankees bought the best player in baseball for $125,000 and a $350,000 loan.

As if buying players weren't good enough, the Yankees scooped up Red Sox manager Ed Barrow following the 1920 season, hiring him as general manager to take care of the team's business affairs. Barrow then systematically plucked players off his former championship team to load up the Yankees.

In 1921, the team acquired Waite Hoyt, who went on to become one of the Yankees' best right-handed pitchers ever. He averaged 16 wins a season in his 10 years with the team, and was elected to the Hall of Fame. That same year saw Wally Schang go from Boston to New York, where he became the everyday catcher for five years, twice hitting over .300.

"Bullet Joe" Bush and "Sad Sam" Jones were acquired for the 1922 season and became regulars in the starting lineup. "Jumpin' Joe" Dugan was brought over that same year, providing the Yankees with a solid hitter and a sparkling fielder at third base.

The Yankees got lefty pitcher Herb Pennock from the Red Sox in 1923 for three no-name players and $50,000. Pennock's career then took off, and he became a mainstay of the club for a decade, twice winning more than 20 games.

And so, the Yankee lineup for its first World Series title in 1923 was loaded with former Red Sox players. In that series, of the starting nine position players, four came from Boston. Even more dramatically, of the five Yankee pitchers who pitched in the World Series, four were former Boston starters. That means that of the 14 primary Yankee players who won the team's first World Series, eight were ex-Red Sox players.

HURRICANE HEARTLESSNESS

Florida was still cleaning up from the death and destruction of Hurricane Frances in September 2004 when the Yankees tried to cash in on Mother Nature's cruel blow to the state.

When the Tampa Bay Devil Rays failed to arrive in New York in time for the start of a scheduled Labor Day doubleheader because of travel problems due to the hurricane, the Yankees had the nerve to ask the commissioner's office to award them a forfeit.

Yankee officials portrayed the team as an innocent victim, saying Major League Baseball rules allow for a forfeit if a team isn't ready within five minutes of umpires calling play unless the delay is unavoidable. Club president Randy Levine said the Devil Rays had an opportunity to fly out of Tampa two or three days before the game—and before the expected hurricane struck.

Devil Ray officials said they stuck by their decision "to stay with our families" during the hurricane and had no intention of flying to New York before the storm hit shore. The commissioner's office agreed, denying the Yankees their ridiculous request.

Tampa Bay manager Lou Piniella, a former Yankee in his playing days, was infuriated. He told reporters that baseball may be important, "but your family is doubly important, or triply important." He said you take care of family first, and baseball comes second.

GRAND(STAND) EXPECTATIONS

Yankee owner George Steinbrenner has had pennants, World Series championships, and loyal fans who come in droves to see the team. But like a spoiled child who doesn't have it all, Steinbrenner has blathered over the years about the shortcomings of Yankee Stadium, one of the most prestigious venues in all of sports.

In the early 1970s, New York City taxpayers were told that Yankee Stadium renovations would cost less than $30 million. The job ended up costing more than $100 million. Two decades later, Steinbrenner was saying he needed more—like a whole new ballpark, in Manhattan, paid for by taxpayers. Or else he'd move the team to New Jersey.

Steinbrenner was joined in the 1990s by then-mayor Rudolph Giuliani, a die-hard Yankees fan who pushed for a new Yankee Stadium on Manhattan's west side. Giuliani, it has been written, had visions of constructing "The House that Rudy Built." The price tag was casually estimated at $1 billion or more.

Steinbrenner, who was born with a silver spoon in his mouth and was now rattling his gold-plated tin cup, had high expectations in his quest. He reminded people that ballparks in other Major League cities had been built with public funds. Taxpayers in Tampa, Florida, had footed the bill for a Yankee spring training stadium. And New York City had provided more than $70 million to help pay for a new park for the Yankees' minor league team on Staten Island.

Predictably, the plans for a new Yankee Stadium have met opposition. After all, Jacob Ruppert paid for the original himself when he owned the team back in 1923. After all, the Yankee franchise is among the most valuable in all of sports. And after all, New York public schools are in need of new roofs and playgrounds.

NEW YORK "DAILY NEWS" SPORTS COLUMNIST MIKE LUPICA WROTE THAT THE ISSUE WAS ABOUT "THE GREED OF THE YANKEE OWNER AND THE ARROGANCE OF THE MAYOR." POLLS SHOWED THAT NEW YORK RESIDENTS, AND YANKEE FANS IN PARTICULAR, OVERWHELMINGLY WANTED THE STADIUM TO STAY PUT.

New York *Daily News* sports columnist Mike Lupica wrote that the stadium issue was about "the greed of the Yankee owner and the arrogance of the mayor." Polls showed that New York residents, and Yankee fans in particular, overwhelmingly wanted the stadium to stay put.

When Steinbrenner made gestures about selling the naming rights of the stadium, public advocate Ralph Nader wrote to Giuliani expressing outrage. "All along, Mr. Mayor, you have supported his agenda to move from the Bronx to Manhattan and to heavily fund the move," Nader wrote in 1998. "You have thrown mayoral dignity out the window for him. And for what? So one of the greediest, stingiest owners of all sports can replace a name so rich in tradition like Yankee Stadium?"

The terrorist attacks of 2001 and their devastating impact on New York City, along with Giuliani's departure from office, slowed down any move to build Steinbrenner a new stadium. But talks have surfaced now and again about the city giving Steinbrenner hundreds of millions of dollars to build a new stadium in the Bronx. The smart money is betting on Steinbrenner getting his way.

CABLE CLASH

When the 2002 baseball season got under way, there was something missing from television sets in the New York area: Yankees' games.

That's because Club Steinbrenner and cable TV giant Cablevision Systems Corp. were going at it tooth and nail in a clash of titanic proportions. The squabble boiled down to this: Greed.

The Yankees Entertainment & Sports Network, or YES, insisted on being offered as a basic cable channel over Cablevision. YES showed most Yankee games and contests from other New York area teams to viewers in New York, Connecticut, and parts of New Jersey and Pennsylvania. Steinbrenner controlled 60 percent of the network, and Goldman Sachs owned a 40 percent stake.

Cablevision head James Dolan and Steinbrenner pointed fingers and called each other names in what amounted to two Evil Empires doing battle. All the while, Yankees fans were deprived of watching their team on the tube.

And so the dispute went on—and on and on and on. Until the season was over.

When the 2003 season opener rolled around, the multimillionaires were still going at it. Barely a week before the opening game, the two sides walked away from the negotiating table, unable to come to an agreement.

Dolan accused YES of "wanting a whole lot more money" and not wanting the case to go to arbitration because they didn't want anybody to see how much money they were making.

It finally took New York attorney general Eliot Spitzer to bring the two sides to an agreement and bring the games back into the homes of the fans. The squabble ended up costing both sides tens of millions of dollars. But in the end—as is usually the case—it would be the fans who would foot the bill.

Eighth Inning

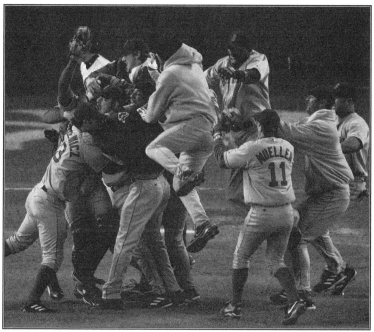

AP Photo

Previous page—The Boston Red Sox celebrate at Yankee Stadium after shocking the Yankees 10–3 in game 7 of the 2004 American League Championship Series to advance to the World Series. The Red Sox became the first team in Major League history to win a seven-game series after trailing three games to none. The following day the New York Daily News neatly summed up the Yankees' 2004 experience: "The Choke's on Us."

THE PLAYOFFS

Major League Baseball instituted a playoff format for the National and American leagues in 1969 by breaking each league into two divisions. The division winners in each league played each other with the winners taking their respective pennants and playing in the World Series. Then in 1994, a third division was added to each league. The three division winners and a wild card team from each league played two rounds of series with the winners going to the World Series.

Since the playoff format was adopted, the Yankees have faltered—sometimes dramatically—in five division and conference series to the likes of the Kansas City Royals, the Seattle Mariners, the Cleveland Indians, the Anaheim Angels and the dreaded Boston Red Sox. Can you say greatest collapse in sports history? Ahhhh, the joy.

2004 AMERICAN LEAGUE CHAMPIONSHIP SERIES
BOSTON (4)
NEW YORK (3)

Just three outs from sweeping their way through the American League Championship Series and into the World Series, the Yankees did what no team had ever done before: They coughed up a seven-game series after holding a 3–0 lead.

It was the ultimate collapse not just in baseball history, but in all of sports. After the loss, New York *Daily News* headlines blared: "Hell Freezes Over" and "The Choke's on Us." The Yankees lost on Yankee Stadium turf before a stunned crowd. All the barrels of money and their excess of ego couldn't help them.

The Yankees had taken the first two games of the Series 10–7 and 3–1, and appeared unbeatable in destroying the Sox, 19–8, in game 3. And in game 4, they were poised to finish off the series when they took a 4–3 lead into the bottom of the ninth. Yankee fans were feeling smug when Mariano Rivera, their ace reliever, took to the mound at Fenway Park.

But he promptly walked leadoff hitter Kevin Millar, and pinch-runner Dave Roberts stole second on the next pitch. Bill Mueller then singled up the middle to drive home Roberts and tie the game. Rivera had just given up the series. Just as dramatically, David Ortiz won it for the Sox in the 12th inning when he pulled a home run to right field for a two-run shot and a 6–4 victory. The seeds were sown for the big choke.

In game 5, the Yankees again let victory slip out of their hands. With the Sox trailing 4–2 in the eighth inning, Ortiz struck again, blasting a one-run shot to cut the lead to 4–3. Then with runners on first and third and no one out, the Yankees brought on Rivera again. Again, he blew the save. Jason Varitek lifted a sacrifice fly to center to knot the game at 4. The teams played into extra innings again when in the 14th, Yankee-killer Ortiz singled home Johnny Damon with the winning run—but only after fighting off pitch after pitch and depositing the 10th pitch of the at bat into center field. The game lasted nearly six hours.

With the Yankees returning home for game 6 and, if needed, game 7, history was on their side. In Major League history, none of the previous 25 teams to fall behind 3–0 in a series had even managed to force a seventh game. In the four major North American sports leagues—Major League Baseball, the NBA, the NFL and the NHL—only two teams had overcome 3–0 deficits in a best-of-7 series to win: the 1942 Toronto Maple Leafs and the 1975 New York Islanders.

But the Yankees made history of their own by losing to Curt Schilling 4–2 in game 6 and then to Derek Lowe in game 7, 10–3, to go down in the record books as the only team to ever squander a 3–0 playoff lead. The Red Sox players danced on the mound of Yankee Stadium.

The Red Sox went on to win their first World Series in 86 years when they met the St. Louis Cardinals. Their momentum in full gear, Boston swept through the Cardinals in four games, never trailing in the series.

Game 4 Final (12)

	1	2	3	4	5	6	7	8	9	10	11	12	R	H	E
NY Yankees	0	0	2	0	0	2	0	0	0	0	0	0	4	12	1
Boston	0	0	0	0	3	0	0	0	1	0	0	2	6	8	0

W: C. Leskanic (1–0) L: P. Quantrill (1–1)

HR: NYY: Rodriguez (3) BOS: Ortiz (2)

2002 AMERICAN LEAGUE DIVISIONAL SERIES
ANAHEIM (3)
NEW YORK (1)

New York with its loaded lineup was the heavy favorite when it faced the Anaheim Angels in the American League divisional series.

The Yankees had won a Major League-best 103 games during the season, and had been to the World Series for four straight seasons, and five out of the past six years. The Angels had never before been in the Fall Classic, and early in the season had been 10.5 games out of first.

It looked like it could be another Yankee rout in the making when the team came back from a late-inning deficit to score four runs in the eighth for an 8–5 series-opening win. The Bronx Bombers had four homers, capped by Bernie Williams's three-run shot in the eighth.

But there'd be no more comebacks.

In game 2, it was the Angels who used eighth-inning heroics—fueled by back-to-back homers by Garrett Anderson and Troy Glaus—to come back and take the game, 8–6.

The Angels kept the bats hot for game 3, erasing a 6–1 deficit for a 9–6 victory. In game 4, Anaheim used an 8-run fifth inning in pounding out 15 hits for the series-clinching 9–5 win.

The Yankees went home, and the Angels went on to the World Series, where they again used come-from-behind heroics to take the World Series in seven games from the San Francisco Giants.

1997 AMERICAN LEAGUE DIVISIONAL SERIES
CLEVELAND (3)
NEW YORK (2)

The Cleveland Indians' record in 1997 was hardly worthy of a playoff team. They were 86–75, winning the crown in the weak Central division, where no other team finished above .500. The Yankees had a 96–66 record for the year, finishing second to Baltimore in the East division.

The Yankees seemed to have some magic left from their World Series win the previous year, when in game 1 they became the first team in postseason history to hit three consecutive home runs, rallying to beat the Indians, 8–6.

In game 2, 21-year-old rookie Jaret Wright survived a rough first inning, and the Indians overcame an early three-run deficit for a 7–5 victory over the Yankees to even their AL playoff series at one game apiece.

Back at home, New York won game 3, 6–1, behind David Wells's five-hitter and Paul O'Neill's grand slam. But the Yankee heroics ended there.

In game 4, Omar Vizquel hit the game-winner off pitcher Ramiro Mendoza's glove in the ninth inning to give the team a 3–2 come-from-behind win. That came an inning after Sandy Alomar tied the game on a homer just out of reach of Paul O'Neill's glove in right field.

The Indians nearly blew a four-run lead in game 5, but held on to put away the series and deny the Yankees a return trip to the World Series. Cleveland went on to beat Baltimore for the American League pennant before falling to the Cinderella Florida Marlins in a seven-game World Series.

1995 AMERICAN LEAGUE DIVISIONAL SERIES
SEATTLE (3)
NEW YORK (2)

The Yankees went into the 1995 playoff as the American League wild card team in their first postseason appearance since 1981. Their opponent was Seattle, which edged out California for the American League West title by a single game.

The Yankees won game 1, 9–6, despite giving up two home runs to Ken Griffey Jr. In the second game, the teams battled back and forth until the Yankees won on Jim Leyritz's two-run homer in the 15th inning.

The Yankees enjoyed a commanding 2–0 series lead heading back to Seattle, while the Mariners needed to win three straight to advance to the League Championship Series. Things looked bleak for Seattle, and the series was the Yankees' to lose.

With ace Randy Johnson pitching, the Mariners grabbed game 3 by a 7–4 score. In the next game, things looked good for the Yankees as they took an early 5–0 lead. But Seattle refused to lose, rallying to win 11–8 behind Edgar Martinez's grand slam, forcing a fifth and deciding game.

In the final seesaw game, the Yankees took a two-run lead into the bottom of the eighth. But the Mariners tied the game at four and forced extra innings. In the top of the 11th inning, the Yankees scored the go-ahead run.

The Mariners refused to roll over with Joey Cora and Griffey hitting singles to bring up Edgar Martinez. With the sellout crowd chanting, "Refuse to Lose," Martinez hit a clutch double down the left-field line to score both Cora and Junior to win the game, 6–5. The crowd, announced at 57,411, went bonkers.

The following day, Major League Baseball fined Yankee owner George Steinbrenner $50,000 for criticizing the umpiring during the series.

1980 AMERICAN LEAGUE CHAMPIONSHIP SERIES
KANSAS CITY (3)
NEW YORK (0)

The Yankees had the Major Leagues' best record in 1980 at 103–59. In the American League Championship Series, they took on the Kansas City Royals, whom the Yankees had dispensed of in 1976, 1977, and 1978 for the pennant.

Although the Yankees had the better record, the Royals had George Brett, who flirted with a .400 average for much of the season before finishing with a .390 average—the highest in the Majors since 1941.

Not only did Brett hit for average, he had power as well, and ended up with 33 doubles, 24 home runs and 118 RBIs. He was the easy MVP choice as the Royals finished 14 games ahead of second-place Oakland in the American League West.

The Royals avenged their earlier playoff losses and swept the Yankees in three straight by scores of 7–2, 3–2 and 4–2. Brett hit two homers and the Royals' pitching had a 1.67 ERA for the series.

The Royals couldn't keep the momentum going, however, and lost to the Philadelphia Phillies in the World Series, 4 games to 2.

". . . I had to confess in my first holy confession that when I said my prayers at night I wished harm to others. Namely, I wished various New York Yankee players would break arms, legs, and ankles so that the Brooklyn Dodgers would win the World Series. I remember the priest asked me, 'How often do you make these horrible wishes?' and I had to admit it was every night."

Doris Kearns Goodwin, Author
Lafayette commencement speech, 2001

NOW BATTING . . .

KEVIN THOMAS

When I hop in the Ford Escort and take the occasional commute from Maine to Yankee Stadium, the routines kick in. I stop along the way, picking up newspapers for research. Before reaching Hartford, I pull into Rein's Deli, right off I-84. Nothing like preparing for a Yankees-Red Sox series than with a true pastrami on rye.

And, finally, for expert analysis and true, logical insight into the Yankees-Red Sox rivalry, I turn on sports talk radio.

On Monday, October 11, 2004, the calls came in from greater Boston. "I really think we can do it this time . . . the curse is over, baby . . . It's, like, destiny, man."

In Connecticut, I switched over to WFAN in New York: "The Yankees win in five. The curse lives on . . . What? Ya kiddin' me? No way the Sox win. No way . . . Boston, they're chokers. Torre, Jeter, Posada. They know how to win."

Not every caller ridicules the Red Sox. You hear New Yorkers acknowledge that the Red Sox have a good team. But it is the patronizing talk of a big brother, knowing that he can beat up his little brother any time he wants to. After a few hours of this, I have reduced the debate to the following: The Yankees win a lot. The Red Sox do not.

There is something about a curse. So, why should 2004 be any different? It will be different, of course, because we're talking baseball games. No two baseball games are alike, let alone seasons.

Outcomes are never predictable—despite the "guarantees" of the sports experts.

Before the Yankees-Red Sox series, reporters approached Boston first-baseman Doug Mientkiewicz. "When I come up and see their 26 world championship [banners], those are not going to get me out," he said. "History has nothing to do with it."

Yankees manager Joe Torre is a baseball man. He can talk about previous Red Sox failures, which had nothing to do with curses or historical precedence.

"If you try to figure out why they haven't won a World Series or gotten into the World Series every time, it's just the lack of depth in their pitching staff," Torre said, "which they do have right now."

But Boston's pitching would struggle and the curse conspiracy theorists were salivating. The Yankees beat Curt Schilling, who was limping on a bad ankle. And they beat Pedro Martinez, who gave one of the more bizarre postgame interviews, talking about his personal evolution from being a teenager in the Dominican Republic "sitting under a mango tree without 50 cents to pay for the bus" to being "the center of attention of the whole city of New York."

Boston was not only losing, but with comments like that of Martinez, they were becoming a joke.

It went from bizarre to outrageous, after the Yankees beat Boston 19–8 in game 3. Knowledgeable sports columnists declared, "It's over." One late-night Boston sports radio host demanded that the "Red Sox apologize to the fans."

Red Sox manager Terry Francona said simply that "We'll show up [for game 4] and our only goal is to win . . . It can look a little daunting if you look at too big a picture."

Too big a picture? This was a colossal landscape. Not only do the Yankees always beat Boston (just ask their fans), but no team ever recovers from an 0–3 deficit. (It's a fact. Ask all those sports geniuses out there.)

Before game 4, Red Sox general manager Theo Epstein walked out of the Boston dugout during batting practice. Media members, with the instinctive senses of any good vulture, surrounded Epstein. How did the Red Sox fail this time? What would he do in the off-season to make Boston more competitive with the Yankees?

Epstein continually tried to steer the conversation to game 4, reminding everyone "that this thing is not finished."

Much later that evening (actually at 1:22 Sunday morning), David Ortiz hit a two-run homer in the bottom of the 12th to win game 4 for Boston. Then came games 5 and 6, and the series was tied 3–3. The much-anticipated game 7 turned into a rout, a 10–3 Boston win.

"When they get on a roll, they can do things, like they did to us," Torre said. "We've always respected their ball club. They're very capable."

In the visitor's clubhouse of Yankee Stadium, champagne and beer flowed, some in mouths, mostly over heads.

"Great things happened today," Johnny Damon said.

"What we did was really, really something," Francona said.

What the Red Sox did was step out of their humble role of little brother and punch big brother in the nose. How did big brother feel?

When I turned on sports radio, on the way back to New England the next day, I listened to the callers from New York. Big brother's brash voice was gone. It took four straight Boston Red Sox wins, but I swear I detected something unique in the callers' tone that day.

Was it humility?

Kevin Thomas covers the Boston Red Sox and Portland Sea Dogs for the Portland (Maine) Press Herald *and* Maine Sunday Telegram, *and previously wrote for the* St. Petersburg Times. *He grew up in St. Petersburg, Florida, where he was known to skip school to watch the New York Mets during spring training.*

Ninth Inning

AP Photo

Previous page—Jackie Robinson of the Brooklyn Dodgers safely steals home in game 1 of the 1955 World Series at Yankee Stadium. Robinson helped "Dem Bums" beat the Yankees 4–3 in the 1955 World Series, erasing years of frustration. Finally, there was no more "Wait till next year" in Brooklyn.

THE WORLD SERIES

The World Series is the Holy Grail of the Major Leagues. A triumph in the Fall Classic is the pinnacle of success not just in baseball, but in all of team sports. And when it comes to the World Series, the championship of our national pastime, there is little doubt that the New York Yankees are in a league of their own.

The Yankees have lost more World Series—13—than any other team in the Major Leagues. That's more series than the Boston Red Sox, the Cleveland Indians, the Chicago White Sox and Baltimore Orioles have lost combined.

The Yankees have been on the losing end of 88 World Series games, by far the most of any team ever. Forty of those were at home, and 48 on the road—both records. In one 10-year span, from 1955 to 1964, they lost a total of 30 World Series games, a feat that stands unmatched to this day (and probably forever).

Bad moments in Yankee Series history date back to 1921, when the boys from the Bronx reached the World Series for the first time. The Yankees lost that series to the New York Giants, 5 games to 3, with a banged-up Babe Ruth striking out eight times and spending most of the series on the bench. They also lost to the St. Louis Cardinals in 1942, 4 games to 1, with undeserving league MVP Joe Gordon submitting a 1-for-21 series and Joe DiMaggio going homer-less while driving in but three runs. And in 1981, the Yankees fell quickly and silently to the Los Angeles Dodgers, 4 games to 2.

In all, the Yankees have been the loser in thirteen World Series. Here are the other ten.

1922 WORLD SERIES
NEW YORK GIANTS (4)
YANKEES (0)

The Yankees were still hurting from their demoralizing loss in the 1921 World Series when they again took on the New York Giants in the second straight Subway Series. But they were full of hope with new acquisitions after raiding the Boston Red Sox and Philadelphia Athletics to solidify their lineup.

The Series had reverted to its best-of-seven format, but the change didn't help the Yankees any, as the Giants took the first game, 3–2, with a three-run eighth inning. The second game ended in a tie, after the umpire made a controversial decision to call the game due to darkness, even though half an hour of sunlight remained.

The Yankees never rebounded, and the Giants swept the last three games for a 4–0–1 sweep. For the Series, the Yankees had a pathetic .203 batting average, with 20 strikeouts and just two homers. Babe Ruth played like the Sultan of Squat, hitting just 2 for 17 for the Series, with a single RBI.

1926 WORLD SERIES
ST. LOUIS CARDINALS (4)
YANKEES (3)

The Yankees were heavy favorites over the St. Louis Cardinals entering the Fall Classic. After all, the Yanks were led by Ruth, who batted .372 with 47 homers, and up-and-comer Lou Gehrig, who hit .313 and 112 RBIs.

After the teams split the first six games, it was Ruth who made the decisive play in the final game. This time, though, it wasn't Ruth's bat that came into play, but rather Ruth's feet and his brain in making a ludicrous decision that ended the Series.

With the Yankees down 3–2 with two outs in the ninth, Ruth drew a walk on a full count, putting cleanup batter Bob Meusel at the plate and giving the Yankee Stadium crowd something to cheer for.

But Meusel never had a chance to tie up the game, as Ruth attempted to steal second base. The slow-footed Bambino was nailed on the throw and tagged out by second baseman Rogers Hornsby. The base-running gaffe ended the Fall Classic, and many fans were irate, believing Ruth's mistake cost the team the Series. They were probably right.

It is the only World Series to this day that came to an end with a base runner being thrown out while attempting to steal.

1955 WORLD SERIES
BROOKLYN DODGERS (4)
YANKEES (3)

"Dem Bums" from Brooklyn were looking for revenge (again) in 1955. The Brooklyn Dodgers and the New York Yankees had met in the World Series five times in the previous 14 years, and the Yankees had won all five. In fact, Brooklyn has been to the World Series seven times and never walked away as champions. Finally, 1955 would be different. There would be no more "Wait till next year."

The Dodgers were led by future Hall of Famers Roy Campanella, Pee Wee Reese, Jackie Robinson and Duke Snider. The teams battled back and forth through six games, forcing a game 7 that pitted Brooklyn's Johnny Podres, the hero of game 3, against game 2 winner Tommy Byrne for the Yankees.

The Dodgers were leading 2–0 going into the bottom of the sixth when the Yankees led off with a walk and a bunt single, putting men on first and second with no outs. The Yankees looked poised to rally and break the Dodgers' hearts once again.

Then came the game's pivotal play: Yogi Berra sliced a long drive just inside the foul pole in left, but little-known Sandy Amoros made a spectacular catch, threw a relay to shortstop Pee Wee Reese, who then hurled the ball to first for a double play that kept anybody from scoring and changed the momentum of the inning.

The game ended 2–0, giving the Dodgers and their working-class fans of Flatbush its first World Championship. Thousands of people took to the streets, cheering, dancing, and weeping. The players celebrated in the clubhouse with Reingold and Schaefer beer and a bit of champagne of undertermined vintage. The team would go to California two years later to become the Los Angeles Dodgers.

1957 WORLD SERIES
MILWAUKEE BRAVES (4)
YANKEES (3)

The Milwaukee Braves were led by Hammerin' Hank Aaron, who hit 44 homers, knocked in 132 runs, and batted .322 in his fourth season in the big leagues. Still, the Yankees—as usual— were an intimidating presence led by team drunk Mickey Mantle, who won his second straight American League MVP award.

It was Don Larsen, the Yankees pitcher who had hurled the first and only perfect game in World Series history the year before, who became the key to the Series. This time around, he was anything but a hero.

In game 7, the well-rested Larsen was called upon to face Lew Burdette, who had won games 2 and 5 for the Braves and was pitching on just two days' rest.

The Braves got the best of Larsen, knocking him out of the game with four runs in the third inning. Burdette, who had been maligned much of his career for throwing spitballs, pitched a seven-hit shutout.

Burdette became the first pitcher to throw two shutouts in a Series since Christy Mathewson did it three times in the 1905 Series. In so doing, he brought Milwaukee its first major professional championship.

AP Photo

The Braves win! Milwaukee Braves Frank Torre (14) jumps on the back of pitcher Lew Burdette as the Braves celebrate a 5–0 victory over the New York Yankees in game 7 to win the 1957 World Series. For the Yankees, the game marks another crushing game 7 loss at Yankee Stadium.

1960 WORLD SERIES
PITTSBURGH PIRATES (4)
YANKEES (3)

The 1960 World Series had the greatest single moment for Yankee haters in World Series history. It can be summed up in two words: Bill Mazeroski.

The Yankees should have won the Series in a blowout, but the plucky Pirates somehow managed to force a game 7. In the final game, the Pirates took a 9–7 lead with five runs in the bottom of the eighth. But the Yankees, with a lineup that included Yogi Berra, Mickey Mantle, Roger Maris, and Tony Kubeck, tied the game with two of their own in the top of the ninth.

So it was on October 13, 1960, with 36,683 fans looking on at Forbes Field, that the Pirates' Bill Mazeroski came to the plate to lead off the bottom of the ninth. On a 1–0 count against Ralph Terry, Mazeroski smashed a long drive over the left-field fence—ending the game in wild celebration as the Yankees watched in disbelief.

"Terry watched the ball disappear, brandished his glove hand high overhead, shook himself like a wet spaniel, and started fighting through the mobs that came boiling from the stands to use Mazeroski like a trampoline," newspaper columnist Red Smith wrote the next day.

For the Yankees, it was a most improbable loss. In the Series, they outscored the Pirates 55–27 and outhit them 91–60. New York had a .338 batting average with 10 home runs, while the Bucs hit just .256 with four round-baggers. The Pirates' pitching staff had an ERA of 7.11, giving up 91 hits in 62 innings. The three New York victories were all lopsided—16–3, 10–0 and 12–0—but the team had failed to put the Series away when it counted.

It's been written that Mickey Mantle cried all the way home to Oklahoma because, he said, the Yankees lost to an inferior team. The Yankees' owners were so upset after the loss that they fired Casey Stengel as manager, even though he had led the Yankees to 10 pennants and seven World Championships.

Game 7 Wednesday, October 13, at Forbes Field, Pittsburgh

	1	2	3	4	5	6	7	8	9	R	H	E
New York	0	0	0	0	1	4	0	2	2	9	13	1
Pittsburgh	2	2	0	0	0	0	0	5	1	10	11	0

NY: Ralph Terry (L, 0–2)
PITT: Harvey Haddix (W, 2–0)
HR: NY: Berra, Skowron
        PITT: Mazeroski, Nelson, Smith

AP Photo

Maz! Jubilant Pittsburgh Pirates fans rush onto Forbes Field in Pittsburgh to congratulate Bill Mazeroski after he hit his famous World Series–winning home run against the New York Yankees in the bottom of the ninth to win game 7, 10–9.

The owners said they released Stengel because of his advancing age, to which Stengel bitterly responded: "I'll never make the mistake of turning 70 again."

1963 WORLD SERIES
LOS ANGELES DODGERS (4)
YANKEES (0)

The 1963 World Series marked the lamest team effort in Yankee World Series history. Facing the Los Angeles Dodgers and their formidable pitching staff, led by Sandy Koufax and Don Drysdale, the Yankees put on a show worthy of a Little League team.

In game 1, Koufax set the tone for the Series as he struck out the first five Yankees to the plate: Kubek, Richardson, Tresh, Mantle and Maris. For the game, Koufax set a Series record with 15 strikeouts in the 5–2 Dodger victory.

Game 2 was more of the same, with the Yankees managing just seven hits in a 4–1 setback. In game 3, Don Drysdale outdueled Jim Bouton for a 1–0 shutout, and Koufax shut them down in the fourth game, 2–1.

It was the first time since 1922 that the Yankees had been swept clean in a World Series. The four runs scored were the fewest by a single team since 1903, when the Philadelphia A's eked out just three. The team batted just .171 for the Series, and the Dodgers' pitchers had a 1.00 ERA. New York players managed just three doubles and two homers, neither of which mattered. Mickey Mantle managed to hit just .133 and drive in a single run.

Despite winning 104 games during the regular season, and having a loaded roster that included MVP Elston Howard, the Yankees didn't lead at any time during the whole Series—not even for an inning.

1964 WORLD SERIES
ST. LOUIS CARDINALS (4)
YANKEES (3)

The 1964 World Series was most notable not for what happened on the field—although the St. Louis Cardinals 4–3 series win is certainly memorable—but for what it signified for the Yankees.

The Yankees were making their fifth straight World Series appearance and their 14th since 1949. But the cracks were showing. The team lost the 1963 World Series and barely hung on to win the 1964 pennant by one game over the Chicago White Sox. Then Bob Gibson and company would drive a stake through the Yankee dynasty.

Between 1921 and 1964, the Yankees appeared in 29 Fall Classics: six in the 1920s, five in the 1930s, five in the 1940s, eight in the 1950s, and they had already been to the Series all five years in the 1960s. But after their fall to the St. Louis Cardinals in seven games, it would take the Yankees 12 more years before they played again in October.

Within two years after the 1964 World Series, the Yankees fell to last place in the American League. This was the last Series appearance for Mickey Mantle, Whitey Ford, Tony Kubek, and Clete Boyer. The day after the Cardinals won game 7 by a score of 7–5, Yogi Berra was fired as manager.

1976 WORLD SERIES
CINCINNATI REDS (4)
YANKEES (0)

The Yankees were out of their class when they took on the Cincinnati Reds in 1976, their first World Series appearance in 12 years—and the first under owner George Steinbrenner, who had bought the team in 1972.

AP Photo

Bob Gibson of the St. Louis Cardinals drives a stake through Evil Empire I in the 1964 World Series. The Cardinals won the series, 4–3. Within two years the Yankees would tumble to a last-place finish, and would not appear in another World Series until 1976.

The Series wasn't even close—the Big Red Machine swept the Yankees in four straight games. You might say it was boring, especially compared to the seven-game thriller in 1975 when the Reds defeated the Red Sox in what is regarded as one of the top World Series of all time.

The men in pinstripes didn't even enjoy a lead until the fourth game, when they scored in the first and led 1–0 for a mere three innings. The Reds so dominated the Series that manager Sparky Anderson didn't make a single change in his batting order or fielding alignment for the entire stretch. The Reds' mighty lineup—Johnny Bench, George Foster, Ken Griffey, Joe

Morgan and Pete Rose among them—batted .313, led by
Bench's .533 and Foster's .429.

It was payback for the Reds, who had been swept by the
Yankees in the 1939 Series. It also marked the first time since
1921 and 1922 that a National League team had won consecutive World Championships.

2001 WORLD SERIES
ARIZONA DIAMONDBACKS (4)
YANKEES (3)

The Arizona Diamondbacks were in just their fourth year of
existence when they made it to the World Series to take on the
Yankees.

The Yankees were shut down in games 1 and 2 by aces Curt
Schilling and Randy Johnson, but came back to win games 3
through 5 by 2–1, 4–3 in 10 innings and 3–2 in 12 innings. In
games 4 and 5, the Yankees scored two runs in the bottom of
the ninth to force extra innings. The Yankee magic seemed to be
at work.

But game 6 wasn't even close—the Diamondbacks trounced
the Yanks, 15–2—setting up a game 7 that would go down as a
dark page in Yankee history.

In the bottom of the ninth, the Yankees led 2–1 with
Mariano Rivera on the mound. Rivera had struck out the side in
the eighth and had converted 23 straight postseason saves, but
he didn't have enough to put away the D-Backs this night.

First Rivera gave up an RBI single that allowed the D-Backs
to tie it. To finish off the game, Luis Gonzalez stepped up with
the Yankees' infield drawn in to prevent base runner Jay Bell
from scoring. Gonzalez blooped a single barely out of reach of
the drawn-in infielders for an improbable 3–2 win over the bul-
lies from the Bronx.

In some fan surveys, the 2001 Series, and game 7 in particular,
is seen as the most disappointing defeat in franchise history.

Game 7
Sunday, November 4 at Bank One Ballpark

	1	2	3	4	5	6	7	8	9	R	H	E
New York	0	0	0	0	0	0	1	1	0	2	6	3
Arizona	0	0	0	0	0	1	0	0	2	3	11	0

NY: Mariano Rivera (L, 0–1)
AZ: Randy Johnson (W, 2–0)
HR: New York, Soriano

2003 WORLD SERIES
FLORIDA MARLINS (4)
YANKEES (2)

Nobody imagined during the regular season that the Florida Marlins would be in the World Series. But somehow the Marlins, who were 10 games under .500 in late May, managed to quietly slip into the Series for the second time in their 10 years of existence.

The Yankees were heavily favored, but it was their pitching that did them in and let Florida win the Series, 4–2. In game 4 with the score knotted at 3 in the 12th inning, manager Joe Torre brought in Jeff Weaver—even though Weaver had been a bust at the end of the season and hadn't pitched in 28 days. The first batter, Alex Gonzalez, lined a full-count pitch down the left-field line, barely clearing the fence for a 4–3 win.

Torre, known for his shrewd decisions, was shredded by fans and the media for deciding to use Weaver in a do-or-die situation.

In the next game, starting pitcher David Wells left with a freak back injury after just one inning. The Marlins then blistered reliever Jose Contreras to take game 5 and go up 3–2.

In the final game, the Yankees' bats came up short, going 0 for 7 with runners in scoring position. Josh Beckett pitched a five-hit complete-game shutout to lead the Marlins over the favored Yankees.

As Marlins' players celebrated their implausible World Series championship, fans in Yankee Stadium were in silent shock as their team let another World Championship slip away.

"I WAS TALKING TO [PITCHER] TERRY MULHOLLAND [IN 1993], AND HE SAID THE AWESOME THING ABOUT BEING A STARTING PITCHER IS YOU HAVE THE ABILITY TO MAKE 55,000 PEOPLE SHUT UP WHEN YOU'RE ON THE ROAD. I'M NOT SURE OF ANY SCENARIO MORE ENJOYABLE THAN MAKING 55,000 PEOPLE FROM NEW YORK SHUT UP."

CURT SCHILLING,
PITCHER, BOSTON RED SOX

A YANKEE HATER'S
TOP TEN YANKEE MOMENTS

Ranking the 10 greatest Yankee moments for Yankee haters everywhere is a tough call. But after much contemplation, here is this man's opinion of the Top Ten:

#10 The 1963 World Series is the most wretched World Series performance ever. Period. Los Angeles Dodgers 4, Yankees 0.

#9 In 1977, Reggie Jackson dons the Yankee cap with the biggest contract in big league history and sets the stage for infighting that earned the team's nickname of the Bronx Zoo.

#8 The 1955 World Series is cause for Yankee haters everywhere to rejoice. Brooklyn Dodgers 4, Yankees 3.

#7 In 1973, pitchers Mike Kekich and Fritz Peterson "lifeswap" by trading wives, children, houses, cars and even the family pets.

#6 The 4-year-old Arizona Diamondbacks steal game 7 of the 2001 World Series to take it all. Diamondbacks 4, Yankees 3.

#5 In 1966, Yankees finish dead last in the American League, 26.5 games out of first.

#4 Owner George Steinbrenner is banned from baseball for life in 1990 for paying a two-bit gambler $40,000 to dig up dirt on Dave Winfield so Steinbrenner wouldn't have to pay the outfielder his due. Alas, the ban lasts only three years.

#3   Boneheaded stealing blunder by Babe Ruth ends the 1926
      World Series with the Yankees on the short end of a seven-
      game series with the St. Louis Cardinals. Cardinals 4,
      Yankees 3.

#2   The Pittsburgh Pirates' Bill Mazeroski hits a homer for the
      ages in the ninth inning of the seventh game and puts the
      Yankees away in the 1960 World Series. Pirates 4, Yankees 3.

And the number-one greatest moment in history for Yankee
haters . . .

THE 2004 AMERICAN LEAGUE CHAMPIONSHIP SERIES

The Yankee breakdown against the Red Sox in the 2004
American League Championship Series was sweeter than sugar.
Not only did the team make history by losing a best-of-7 series
after leading 3–0, but they did it with such style.

The beauty of the series was that, unlike a home run or a bad
game that occurs over a matter of a few seconds or a few hours,
the team's collapse amounted to Chinese water torture for
Yankee fans. Their failure was spread over five days—pitch by
pitch, hit by hit, inning by inning—like a car crash happening
in slow motion right before their eyes.

The collapse was all the sweeter in that it ended in Yankee
Stadium in front of incredulous Yankee fans, whose smugness
was erased from their faces as they sat in stunned silence.

AP Photo

Yankee-killer David Ortiz after driving home the winning run in game 5 of the 2004 American League Championship Series won by the Red Sox, 4–3. The Red Sox became the first team in baseball history to win a seven-game series after trailing three games to none.

Off-season

AP Photo

Previous page—Cincinnati Reds catcher Johnny Bench scores after hitting a home run in the 1976 World Series against the Yankees. The Big Red Machine swept the Yankees to win the Series.

YANKEE TIMELINE

1903 Frank Farrell and Bill Devery, a gambling kingpin and a former corrupt police commissioner, buy the defunct Baltimore franchise and move the team to New York. They build Hilltop Park, a sorry excuse for a stadium, and begin play as the Highlanders. They lose their first game, 3–1, at Washington.

1912 Pinstripes first appear on the team uniforms, and the club finishes with a record of 50–102, a .329 winning percentage. It is the worst record in franchise history.

1913 The franchise becomes known as the Yankees and begins playing its games at the Polo Grounds, which it shares with the New York Giants of the National League.

1915 Col. Jacob Ruppert and Col. Tillinghast L'Hommedieu "Cap" Huston purchase the team—even though both men are admitted Giants fans.

1921 The Yankees lose to the Giants, 5–3, in their first World Series appearance.

1922 The team is swept in the World Series, 4–0, by the Giants.

1923 Yankee Stadium opens with a crowd of 74,200. Babe Ruth hits the first home run in the new stadium.

1923 The franchise wins its first World Series, 4–2, against the Giants.

1926   The Yankees lose the World Series, 4–3, to the St. Louis Cardinals. The Series ends when Babe Ruth is caught stealing.

1934   The Yankees release Babe Ruth after he hits only 22 homers. He goes to the Boston Braves for the next season, where he plays just 28 games, hitting six homers and batting .181.

1939   Lou Gehrig's consecutive game streak of 2,130 comes to an end.

1941   Joe DiMaggio hits in 56 consecutive games.

1942   The Cardinals beat the Yankees, 4–3, in the World Series.

1945   Del Webb, Dan Topping and Larry MacPhail purchase the team from the estate of the late Col. Jacob Ruppert. Webb and Topping buy out MacPhail's share two years later.

1955   The Brooklyn Dodgers beat the Yankees, 4–3, in the World Series.

1956   Yankee pitcher Don Larsen throws the only perfect game ever in World Series history.

1957   The Milwaukee Braves defeat the Yankees, 4–3, in the World Series.

1960   Bill Mazeroski hits a ninth-inning, seventh-game homer to lead the Pittsburgh Pirates to a World Series victory over the Yankees.

1963   The Yankees put on a pitiful hitting display as the Los Angeles Dodgers sweep the World Series.

1964   The Cardinals win the World Series, 4–3, over the Yankees.

1964   CBS purchases 80 percent of the franchise for $11.2 million, and later buys the remaining 20 percent.

1966   The team finishes in last place in the American League for the first time in 54 years. Attendance falls to its lowest level in 20 years.

1972   Attendance drops to 966,328, the first time since World War II that it dips below 1 million.

1973 A partnership headed by George Steinbrenner buys the franchise. Steinbrenner says he won't be active in day-to-day operations of the team.

1973 Pitchers Mike Kekich and Fritz Peterson announce they are "life-swapping" by trading wives, children, houses, cars and even the family pets.

1974 Steinbrenner pleads guilty to making illegal campaign contributions to Richard Nixon and is fined $20,000. He is suspended from the league for two years.

1974 The Yankees begin the first of two seasons they'll play at Shea Stadium while Yankee Stadium undergoes renovations.

1976 The Cincinnati Reds sweep the Yankees in the World Series.

1981 The Dodgers win four straight games in beating the Yankees in the World Series, 4–2.

1983 The Yankees and Royals play the infamous "pine tar game" where George Brett's home run is waved off after Yankee manager Billy Martin objects to the amount of pine tar on Brett's bat.

1990 Commissioner Fay Vincent bans Steinbrenner for life from running the Yankees after it's revealed that he paid a gambler $40,000 to find dirt on Dave Winfield. The ban is overturned three years later when baseball owners fire Vincent.

1995 The Seattle Mariners overcome a 2–0 game deficit to beat the Yankees, 3–2, in the American League Division Series.

2001 The Arizona Diamondbacks score two runs in the bottom of the ninth of Game 7 to beat the Yankees in the World Series.

2003 The Yankees lose the World Series, 4–2, to the Florida Marlins.

2004 In the most colossal collapse in team sports history, the Yankees lose to the Red Sox in the American League Championship Series after leading the series three games to none.

SELECTED READING

Anderson, Dave, Murray Chass, Robert Creamer, and Harold Rosenthal. *The Yankees: The Four Fabulous Eras of Baseball's Most Famous Team*. New York: Random House, 1979.

Angell, Roger. *The Summer Game*. New York: The Viking Press, 1972.

Barber, Red. *1947: When All Hell Broke Loose in Baseball*. Garden City, NY: Doubleday & Co., 1987.

Bashe, Philip. *Dog Days: The New York Yankees' Fall From Grace and Eventual Return to Glory, 1964–1976*. New York: Random House, 1994.

Bouton, Jim. *Ball Four*. New York: World Publishing Co., 1970.

Castro, Tony. *Mickey Mantle: America's Prodigal Son*. Washington, D.C.: Brassey's Inc., 2002.

Chadwin, Dean. *Those Damn Yankees: The Secret Life of America's Greatest Franchise*. New York: Verso Press, 1999.

Charlton, James. *The Baseball Chronology: The Complete History of the Most Important Events in the Game of Baseball*. Old Tappan, New Jersey: Macmillan Publishing, 1991.

Cramer, Richard Ben. *Joe DiMaggio: The Hero's Life*. New York: Simon & Schuster, 2000.

Creamer, Robert. *Babe: The Legend Comes to Life*. New York: Simon & Schuster, 1974.

Danzig, Allison, and Joe Reichler. *The History of Baseball*. Englewood Cliffs, NJ: Prentice-Hall Inc., 1959.

Dewey, Donald, and Nicholas Acocella. *The Biographical History of Baseball*. New York: Carroll & Graf Publishers Inc., 1995.

Frommer, Harvey. *Baseball's Greatest Rivalry: The New York Yankees and Boston Red Sox*. New York: Atheneum, 1982.

Gentile, Derek. *The Complete New York Yankees: The Total Encyclopedia of the Team*. New York: Black Dog & Leventhal Publishers, 2004.

Honig, Donald. *Baseball America*. New York: Macmillan Publishing Co., 1985.

Honig, Donald. *The New York Yankees*. New York: Crown Publishers, 1981.

Kahn, Roger. *The Era: 1947–1957, When the Yankees, the Giants and the Dodgers Ruled the World*. New York: Houghton Mifflin Co., 1993.

Lally, Richard. *Bombers: An Oral History of the New York Yankees*. New York: Crown Publishers, 2002.

Leventhal, Josh. *The World Series: An Illustrated Encyclopedia of the Fall Classic*. New York: Tess Press, 2004.

Lyle, Sparky and Peter Golenbock. *The Bronx Zoo*. New York: Crown Publishers, 1979.

Madden, Bill and Moss Klein. *Damned Yankees: A No-Holds-Barred Account of Life with "Boss" Steinbrenner*. New York: Warner Books, 1990.

Nettles, Graig, and Peter Golenbock. *Balls*. New York: G.P. Putnam's Sons, 1984.

Palmer, Pete, and Gary Gillette. *The Baseball Encyclopedia*. New York: Barnes & Noble Books, 2004.

Pepitone, Joe. *Joe, You Coulda Made Us Proud*. New York: Dell Publishing Co., 1975.

Schlossberg, Dan. *The New Baseball Catalog*. Middle Village, NY: Jonathan David Publishers Inc., 1998.

Wagenheim, Kal. *Babe Ruth: His Life and Legend*. New York: Henry Holt & Co., 1974.

Wallace, Joseph (ed.). *The Baseball Anthology*. New York: Henry N. Abrams Inc. Publishers, 1994.

Ward, Geoffrey C. and Ken Burns. *Baseball: An Illustrated History*. New York: Alfred A. Knopf, 1994.

Wells, David. *Perfect I'm Not: Boomer on Beer, Brawls, Backaches and Baseball*. New York: William Morrow, 2003.

Zoss, Joel and John Bowman. *The American League: A History*. New York: Gallery Books, 1986.

SELECTED WEB SITES

Babe Ruth Museum: www.baberuthmuseum.com
Baseball Almanac: www.baseball-almanac.com
Baseball Library.com: www.baseballlibrary.com
Baseball Historian.com: www.baseballhistorian.com
Boston Red Sox: http://boston.redsox.mlb.com
ESPN: www.espn.com
Major League Baseball: www.mlb.com
New York Yankees: http://newyork.yankees.mlb.com
The Baseball Page: www.thebaseballpage.com
The Sports Network: www.sportsnetwork.com
Yankee Tradition: www.yankeetradition.com

ABOUT THE AUTHOR

Clarke Canfield is a native of Boston and comes from a long line of Yankee haters. He got his start in journalism at the *Courier News* in Blytheville, Arkansas, and later worked at the *Nashville Banner* and the *Portland* (Maine) *Press Herald.* He now works for The Associated Press.

Canfield has been an editor at three different magazines and has written free-lance articles for a number of publications, including *The Washington Post, The Dallas Morning News* and *San Francisco Chronicle.* This is his first book.

Photo by Robert F. Bukaty

He has a bachelor's degree from the University of Denver and a master's in journalism from Boston University. He lives in South Portland, Maine, with his wife, Amy, and their son, Eli.